W9-DCB-705

Praise for
The Essential Performance Review Handbook

"Sharon has written a straight forward, concise handbook that gets at the heart of performance reviews. The tips, techniques, management principles, and common sense she provides will help managers and employees make performance reviews more effective."

—Vern Schellenger, vice president of human resources and organizational development, American Association of Motor Vehicle Administrators

"*The Essential Performance Review Handbook* turns the writing of such appraisals from a tedious paperwork chore to a powerful management and motivational tool—a valuable new way of thinking about an old task.

—Robert W. Bly, author, *101 Ways to Make Every Second Count*

"Here's a practical, easy-to-use guide to performance appraisal that's valuable to employee and supervisor alike. Continuing case studies allow us to see the whole range of performance management. It's a gem of good writing and sound advice from a wise author who knows her stuff."

—Dick Grote, author, *The Complete Guide to Performance Appraisal* and *The Performance Appraisal Question and Answer Book*

"This book is a terrific resource! It's solid, well-written, full of relevant examples, and sample forms. It should be on the shelf of every good HR professional."

—Mary Walter Midkiff, SPHR, director, talent management, SCA Americas, LLC

"Sharon Armstrong's recent book about Performance Appraisals provides valuable information to managers and employees who support high organizational performance and top-notch individual and team development. The book's format makes it easy to come away with quick tips and great ideas that make a sometimes stressful process much less so. The book is especially useful because it provides guidance to both managers and employees, along with relevant examples. It is also a great resource for HR professionals."

—Jacqueline Basile, vice president, human resources, WETA

"Sharon Armstrong has once again presented important information in a concise and clear manner that any manager, experienced or new to the responsibilities, will find most helpful. For those of us with years of experience it is a terrific reminder of things that might not be forefront in our thoughts as we confront a form that must be completed on a tight deadline. The discussion in Chapter 6 is a terrific reminder of the many ways errors can creep into the rating process. Everyone should review these 16 rating traps prior to beginning the preparation of any review."

—Eugenia Burkes, director of administration, Mayer Brown LLP

"Sharon Armstrong's new book on performance appraisal provides both the theory as well as the practicality of this challenging managerial process. Throughout the book, Armstrong suggests useful checklists addressing the process from the perspectives of the employee and the supervisor. The performance appraisal is viewed as a team process with each player (employee and supervisor) having their own role and responsibilities but focused on the common objective: two-way communication. If you, like most of us, could use some useful guidance in this process, this is the book to use."

—Michael Strand, president, HR Dynamics, Inc.

"It is no surprise that a great deal of anxiety surrounds the performance appraisal process for managers and employees alike. *The Essential Performance Review Handbook* delivers an impact. Through its pages we are reminded of the 'why and how' of delivering a performance review as it was intended—managing to employee strengths with the art of providing constructive feedback. Upon completion of this handbook, we embrace the next opportunity to conduct a review with a renewed sense of purpose in doing so."

—Kathy Albarado, CEO, Helios HR

"As President and CEO of an HR consulting firm, I strongly recommend this book. It is a comprehensive and valuable business tool that will help your organization improve relations with your employees and lead to greater contributions from your staff."

—Mark Stevenson, president, Smart HR, Inc.

"As HR Director at a Washington, D.C. trade association, I've had to prepare PowerPoint and training presentations around the subject of performance reviews, so I thought I've seen and heard it all. That was until I read *The Essential Performance Review Handbook*. Sharon Armstrong has done a great job at capturing the essentials enhanced with sidebars, examples, and checklists that work for everyone. This book is a must read for anyone that wants to improve their performance evaluation and review experience."

—Paul McGee, director, human resources,
American Health Care Association

"Sharon Armstrong captures the key elements of effective feedback in this concise summary of the challenges of preparing, writing, and presenting a performance review. Extensive references to thought leaders provide helpful perspective. Sample interactions with employees at different performance levels create a "how to" outline for a workplace leader faced with the challenge of completing a review form to satisfy the demands of an HR system. Written around a consistent theme that a review summarizes a series of interactions, the book also provides key insights to understand the HR principles that are too often misunderstood and become road blocks to effective feedback."

—Mike Deblieux, SPHR, principal consultant, author of *Performance Appraisal Sourcebook* and *The Supervisor's Guide to Employee Performance Reviews*

"*The Essential Performance Review Handbook* is the perfect desktop tool for managers. It provides great insight on the importance of approaching the review process as an on-going dialogue vs. a one-time event. The real-life scenarios and assessment tools are extremely helpful. This is a must-read for everyone involved in the review process!"

—Jennifer Clinton, COO, The Washington Center for Internships and Academic Seminars

"Sharon presents a variety of straight-forward tips and suggestions for the novice supervisor, the more experienced managers and for employees themselves. Taking her "self-assessment for supervisors" is a quick way to refresh some of the areas that are important in a supervisor's role in managing performance. A good reminder! Sharon also provides useful guidance for addressing performance and compensation in tight economic times – a very timely commentary. Once again, a practical guide for both managers and employees!"

—Naomi Morales, vice president, administration and human resources, PhRMA

"A tremendous mix of authentic case studies, information, and skills discussion support a truly clear and functional tool for BOTH managers and employees. This work creates a new perspective of the appraisal process, moving the readers understanding of performance appraisals from a focus on a written form to a recognition of the same as a process which serves as an essential cog supporting the larger organizational system."

—Madelyne L. D'Angelo, director, human resources operations, L-3 Enterprise IT Solutions

"There are plenty of books around that address performance reviews, but this is that rare book that provides both very practical advice and thought-provoking commentary. It is apparent that Ms. Armstrong has a very deep understanding of the performance review process and its wider role in human resources management. *The Essential Performance Review Handbook* should be required reading for new managers and seasoned pros alike."

—Joyce Oliner, Principal, Oliner Consulting

"Contrary to what the song says, time is not on our side. *The Essential Performance Review Handbook* paves the road with useful information that managers can use immediately. The book is easy to read. I love the format, especially the side bar inserts. Sharon Armstrong writes clearly and with impact. The book is the right prescription for PRAD—Performance Review Anxiety Disorder. Read it and use it, the only side effect is improving your management effectiveness."

—Michel P. Mathieu, senior human resources consultant,
Inova Fairfax Hospital

"*The Essential Performance Review Handbook* takes the established practice of performance management and evolves it to a contemporary practice blueprint. Performance management, like all management practices, must align with worker values and the era during which they live. Many of the other performance management resources available are stale and reflect practices from the past. This is a modern, concise, user-friendly manual I will highly recommend to those who are committed to truly making a difference through the science and art of performance management.

—Christine Peterson, associate vice president/chief human resources officer,
The Catholic University of America

"*The Essential Performance Review Handbook* is a how-to guide that makes simple work out of a complex subject. Sharon Armstrong's conversational writing style makes this an easy read and helps you envision how you might incorporate some of these principles to train managers and employees and enhance your review process. It helps identify our humanity as part of the process, highlights awareness to possible reviewer errors of subjectivity and how we unconsciously can err. The case examples and exercises provide useful tools to illustrate Armstrong's key points and offer an excellent means to instruct your internal audience, whether supervisor or employee."

—Diane I. Bessette, office manager/human resource generalist,
National Association of Public Hospitals and Health Systems

"This is the perfect book for emerging supervisors as well and the seasoned manager. Chapter 9, which discusses performance reviews in a changing world, was spot on! It talks to the challenges of the virtual teams, telecommuting, and job sharing, which are more of a reality in today's business world then ever before. This is one of the only performance review handbooks where I've seen information on the generational differences and how they each perceive the process of feedback..... This book will become a core reference for our management staff."

—Sheri Leonardo, senior vice president, human resources,
Ogilvy Public Relations Worldwide

The Essential Performance Review Handbook

By Sharon Armstrong

CAREER
PRESS

Pompton Plains, NJ

Copyright © 2010 by Sharon Armstrong

All rights reserved under the Pan-American and International Copyright Conventions. This book may not be reproduced, in whole or in part, in any form or by any means electronic or mechanical, including photo-copying, recording, or by any information storage and retrieval system now known or hereafter invented, without written permission from the publisher, The Career Press.

THE ESSENTIAL PERFORMANCE REVIEW HANDBOOK
EDITED AND TYPESET BY DIANA GHAZZAWI
Cover design by Jeff Piasky
Printed in the U.S.A.

To order this title, please call toll-free 1-800-CAREER-1 (NJ and Canada: 201-848-0310) to order using VISA or MasterCard, or for fur-ther information on books from Career Press.

The Career Press, Inc., 220 West Parkway, Unit 12
Pompton Plains, NJ 07444
www.careerpress.com

Library of Congress Cataloging-in-Publication Data
Armstrong, Sharon, 1951-
    The essential performance review handbook : a quick and handy resource for any manager or HR professional / by Sharon Armstrong.
        p. cm.
    Includes bibliographical references and index.
    ISBN 978-1-60163-113-8 -- ISBN 978-1-60163-744-4 (ebook)
    1. Employees--Rating of--Handbooks, manuals, etc. 2. Performance standards--Handbooks, manuals, etc. I. Title.

HF5549.5.R3A7596 2010
658.3'125--dc22

                                                2010008879

Dedication

This book is dedicated to Madelyn Appelbaum and Irene Cardon, two friends who bravely traveled this road with me before.

Acknowledgments

My sincere thanks to Anne Goodfriend, my true partner and the best editor I know; Susan Devereaux, a skilled, tireless, thorough, and smart virtual assistant; Diane Gold, a sound and generous legal source; Marilyn Allen, a literary agent who is simply wonderful; and Richard, my rock.

Additional shout-outs go to Irene Cardon, Erin Curran, Amy Dufrane, Wendi Eldh, Helen Elmore, Gayle George, Allyn Gutauskas, Amanda Haddaway, Bob Kline, Margaret Lack, Natalie Loeb, Julie Perez, Nancy Rawles, Louise Rosenbaum, Pamela Ross, Vern Schellenger, Stephanie Simpson, Priscilla Vazquez, and Yvonne Zhou.

In the words of William Butler Yeats, "Think where man's glory most begins and ends, and say my glory was I had such friends."

Contents

Introduction

It's Not Supposed to Be This Way...

Performance appraisals can be one of the most anxiety-provoking aspects of work life—for both supervisors and employees. Appraisals are meant to clarify and reward, and to be interactive and fair. They take real time, real dialogue, and a real focus on the future, rather than just the previous months. And they need to work successfully for all employees—not just the terrific ones!

Yet, that's not how they often work. Supervisors tell of too much focus on tedious written forms and too little training in how to use them, of "just getting through it," of getting hit with complaints or lawsuits when there's even a hint about "improvement opportunities," and of the difficulties of measuring intangibles. Employees often just plain dread appraisals, citing feelings of trepidation from a "once-a-year necessary evil," anger about having one error dragged through 10 categories, and frustration with "perfunctory" appraisals that neither acknowledge nor foster growth. As one employee put it, "The perception of the individual or relationship often dictates how critical or complementary a supervisor will be."

Why does one of the most vital and continuing workplace responsibilities so often show a shabby face? A 2006 survey by the Council of Communication Management confirmed what almost every employee already knows—that positive feedback related to their efforts and recognition for a job well done are the top motivators of employee performance. Via formal evaluations and regular informal routes, performance appraisals yield excellent opportunities to motivate. Yet the process is frequently counterproductive, or viewed merely as perfunctory.

According to the United Kingdom's Institute of Personnel and Development, one in eight managers would prefer to visit the dentist than carry out a performance appraisal.[1] It's not supposed to be this way. Rather than a painful yearly event, performance evaluations can be viewed as a culmination of small meetings, formal and informal, held throughout the evaluation period. They can be shaped objectively, according to clear standards for employee performance. They can clarify present expectations, track future ones, and underscore the importance of two-way feedback. They can help engage employees in their own career development.

Happily, the elements involved—goal setting, effective observation, practical documentation, and ongoing communications—can all be learned. In this book, you'll find sound guidelines, sample evaluation forms, and helpful insights for use on both sides of the desk. There are critical do's and don'ts, tips for "owning" the appraisal, and ways to leverage it.

In one form or another, performance reviews will continue to be a fact of our work life. This book is designed to cut through the anxiety and make the process more productive and less unpleasant. It's also designed to bring performance appraisals into the 21st century, including such areas as job-sharing, telecommuting, shared supervision, team evaluations, nerve-wracking economic forecasts, legal concerns, and accommodating particular employee challenges. The chapters tap into the actual feelings of employees and their bosses. You'll find good examples and painful ones, real-life performance-review problems and guidance in handling them.

Participating in your formal evaluation sessions need no longer be one of the worst days of your year at work.

1

The Roots of Anxiety

No matter how "scientific," no matter even how many insights it produces, an appraisal that focuses on "potential," on "personality," on "promise"—on anything that is not proven and provable performance—is an abuse.

—Peter Drucker, management guru

Enter the fast heartbeat. Although so many of us have experienced performance reviews for years—often on both sides of the desk—even asking about them usually raises blood pressure. These discussions and forms—called reviews, evaluations or appraisals—tend to be seen as negative experiences by both supervisors and their staffs. Whether glowing or, more often, just pro forma, they conjure up images of "being called to the principal's office," "getting hit with a bad surprise," or "engaging in a sham." One supervisor worried about being "perceived as the enemy" because she gave a candid review. A mid-level employee said he wanted "constructive criticism" but was anxious because he didn't know what it would be. One employee simply said, "I hate being judged, and that's all appraisals really are."

Performance appraisals are an important element of performance management, although their criteria and formats vary widely. Conducted yearly or semi-annually, these formal interactions between employees and their direct supervisors point out employees' strengths and weaknesses, and include assessing the achievement of previous goals and setting new ones for the employees to work toward.

Ideally, the review is a two-way discussion, and the employee's strengths and weaknesses are considered within the context of the organization's mission. Ideally, the performance review is constructive, separate from discussion of compensation, and contains no surprises. It should reflect a series of discussions or mini-reviews that have been conducted throughout the year.

For good reason, in *The Practice of Management*, Peter Drucker writes that discussion of financial rewards should be postponed until nearly the end of the process: "Financial rewards are not major sources of positive motivation in the modern industrial society, even though discontent with them inhibits performance. The best economic rewards are not substitutes for responsibility or for the proper organization of the job."[1] It appears best to postpone discussion about pay until after the review, as it can divert attention from the work itself.

Though supervisors and their staffs employ every mode of avoidance when faced with appraisals, the evaluation inevitably occurs, even if it's six months late.

It doesn't help that there's a dramatic disconnect between what tends to count most to employees and what supervisors *think* counts most to employees. Despite changing conditions, studies first conducted by the Labor Relations Institute of New York in 1946, then repeated in 1981 and 1994, reinforced the conclusion that the most-valued factor to white-collar, non-supervisory employees was "full appreciation for work done," followed closely by feeling "in on" things. In 1946, those values ranked first and second respectively; they eased into second and third place, respectively, in 1981 and 1994, when "interesting work" topped the list. In all three studies, "good wages" ranked fifth of 10 factors. When immediate supervisors were asked what motivated their employees, they ranked good wages first, job security second and

Supervisors' Perspectives

- ✓ Delivering bad news is painful.
- ✓ There's never time to prepare.
- ✓ It's hard to measure intangibles.
- ✓ There's no accountability, so why bother.
- ✓ There's no training or guidance.
- ✓ There's forced ranking—the bell curve is more important than the employees.
- ✓ Required forms outweigh the St. James Bible.
- ✓ Employees only want to get to the money part.
- ✓ It's hard to distinguish between criticism and professional development.
- ✓ Employees may come up with surprises.
- ✓ It's tough to be objective about employees you like.

Employees' Perspectives

- ✓ It's a meaningless exercise.
- ✓ Emphasis is on form, not process.
- ✓ Surprises are scary.
- ✓ They're always late, even when raises are attached.
- ✓ Supervisors just want to get through them.
- ✓ There's always one negative area, then little about anything else.
- ✓ It's never a two-way discussion.
- ✓ The basis for measurement is unclear.
- ✓ A "meets expectations" rating is like getting a "C"...no matter what my supervisor says.
- ✓ My boss has no real understanding of what I do every day.

promotion/growth opportunities third,[2] a ranking that stayed constant in all three studies.[3] With such wide variance, it is not surprising that employees are often less certain about where they stand after the appraisal than before it, tend to evaluate supervisors less favorably afterward, and often report that few constructive actions or significant improvements resulted. In 2001, an international survey of 8,000 employees and managers revealed that fully one-third of employees reported receiving little or no assistance in improving their performance, that they had never even had a formal discussion with their managers regarding overall performance.[4]

It is not only employees who disparage evaluation practices. Managers cite performance appraisals as the task they dislike the most, second only to firing an employee.[5] As a longtime giver and receiver of performance reviews once said, "As an employee, I'd rather be in the dentist's chair. As a supervisor, I think, 'Isn't there something more important to do today...like budget planning? Despite careful preparation, I'm always afraid I'll screw the appraisal up.'"

But evaluations are a serious personal and organizational matter. Every performance appraisal that fails to motivate—or worse, demoralizes—is a lost opportunity for both the employee and the employer. Each employee evaluation that neglects to recognize actual employee performance perpetuates weaker qualities and fails to reinforce the positive. Morale, employee esteem and organizational interests suffer in the process. One banking employee said her perfunctory annual review only reinforced that she was a "9-to-5 fixture and not a real human being." She advanced quickly when she joined a wiser financial institution.

Early career issues are a sensitive matter, too. Though young people are often disappointed by the nature of their first work assignments at the bottom of an organization, they still believe they are doing a good job. Therefore, many are surprised and disappointed by their initial performance appraisals because their managers focus primarily on the areas most in need of correction.[6] Thus, these young employees sour on the process from the start.

The following pages are designed to help change that initial reaction, to help you step back from particular incidents and concerns and focus on the broader, brighter picture.

Why Do Performance Appraisals?

- ✓ Two-way performance feedback.
- ✓ Recognition for individual performance.
- ✓ Motivational tool when used effectively.
- ✓ Goal-setting for next review period in context of organizational/departmental needs.
- ✓ Opportunity to reinforce and document personnel decisions.
- ✓ Opportunity to demonstrate organizational fairness to all employees.
- ✓ Opportunity to support individual needs.
- ✓ Opportunity to reinforce continuing open communication and strengthen rapport.
- ✓ Opportunity to both spur independent thinking and encourage teamwork.
- ✓ Opportunity to encourage employees to take responsibility for their work.
- ✓ Opportunity to contribute to organizational effectiveness.
- ✓ Opportunity to discover untapped potential on both sides of the desk.

These self-assessments are designed to pinpoint areas of particular interest or concern. Certain responses may serve as a wake-up call, providing insight that can help you focus on these areas in the following chapters.

Self-Assessment for Supervisors

How do you rate yourself on the following?

(1 = very often; 5 = not at all)

Provide timely feedback on a regular basis.	
Carefully plan and prepare for the performance appraisal discussion.	
Hold the performance discussion when it's expected.	
Pull specific examples to support ratings.	
Ensure that all appraisal discussions are private and confidential.	
Set aside an appropriate amount of time to have a meaningful exchange.	
Let my employees know how much I value their work.	
Have a clear understanding of my organization's mission/goals.	
Review the completed form for fairness prior to the meeting.	
Encourage two-way communication.	
Take into account my employees' needs and goals as we plan the future.	
Offer viable suggestions for improvement and development.	
Separate the discussion of performance from talk about raises or other compensation.	
I clearly communicate expectations to my employees, given my previous responses.	

Average your ratings.

If average is 1: Outstanding performance that shows up in exceptional accomplishments of both you and your staff. You are an inspiration to your staff.

If average is 2: Performance consistently meets and often exceeds requirements. Teamwork is usually accomplished in a highly effective way. You sometimes motivate employees.

If average is 3: Minimal expected. You get the job done.

If average is 4: Needs are being addressed inconsistently. Established requirements are not being met. Work tends to get done, but sometimes with less than complete effectiveness. Staff rarely receives recognition.

If average is 5: Performance is unacceptable. Established requirements are not being met.

Self-Assessment for Employees

How do you rate yourself on the following?

(1 = very often; 5 = not at all)

Meet my yearly objectives.	
Complete work assignments on time.	
Make contributions to work group.	
Work effectively with coworkers to accomplish department goals.	
Share important work information with others.	
Talk to my supervisor when I need help.	
Express interest in new challenges.	
Make an effort to learn about my organization's goals and how I can advance them.	
Assist my boss without being asked.	
Assist my coworkers without being asked.	
Openly review my work to learn how I can improve.	
Make an effort to build bridges with other departments.	
Ask for feedback on several levels.	

Average your ratings:

If average is 1: Outstanding performance that results in exceptional accomplishments. You are an extremely conscientious employee.

If average is 2: Performance consistently meets and frequently exceeds requirements. Work is accomplished in a highly effective manner.

If average is 3: Minimal expected level of performance. You are getting the job done.

If average is 4: Performance does not consistently meet established requirements. Duties and responsibilities are accomplished, but sometimes with less than complete effectiveness. Improvement is required. It would be wise to seek on-the-job guidance.

If average is 5: Performance is unacceptable and does not meet established requirements. Key responsibilities are not being fulfilled. Improved performance is necessary and must be sustained for successful employment. On-the-job guidance is vital.

2

Forget Winging It!

Understanding should precede judging.

—Louis D. Brandeis,
U.S. Supreme Court Justice 1916–1939

Winging a performance review isn't the answer. It almost guarantees morale, management, and legal dilemmas, and inconsistency from one department to another. Not only is it counterproductive, it impedes an organization's mission and goals.

Given that performance appraisals are a fact of 21st-century work life, and bound to come in widely diverse shapes and sizes that are most often handed to you, the best way to deal with them is to be clear—*before* the evaluation—about who you are evaluating, what you are evaluating, and why your appraisal is geared in one direction or another, bolstered by objective, legally sound examples.

As a hallmark of effective performance management, performance appraisals rarely work well on the fly. Being prepared makes the difference between an uninformed appraisal that's frustrating, futile, and possibly legally hazardous, and one that elevates shared understanding, communication, and, within the framework of clear goals, achievements during the next evaluation cycle and beyond. What's really needed is a review before the review, a solid checklist that will make the whole review process smoother, more productive, and legally defensible.

How to Prepare

Know your employee or your supervisor. If you're an employee whose supervisor doesn't often open the door, take the initiative yourself and make an appointment to talk to him or her periodically. Angst comes when the performance review is the single time, or just one of few times, that supervisors and employees sit down together during the year. One organization asked its employees to complete the appraisal form themselves—in the third person. The employees felt duped, believing that their supervisors didn't care enough to even fill out the form. Optimally, a performance evaluation wraps up a series of informal discussions held throughout the year, serving as a springboard to move forward with new ideas, improved performance, and perhaps more responsibility.

Knowing your supervisor or employee means being better able to anticipate his or her reaction to your comments, and then "managing" your responses to generate positive results. Managers' effectiveness is significantly influenced by insight into their own work. Those who can be introspective about their work are likely to be effective at their jobs.[1] Employees seek not just success but also gratification.

Demonstrate respect and confidentiality. How, when, and even whether appraisals are conducted send a strong message. When a supervisor delays appraisals, does them on the fly, allows interruptions during the review session, doesn't have paperwork complete, or generally doesn't demonstrate that the evaluation is a priority, an employee may feel that he or she isn't, either. If an employee shows up late, participates only half-heartedly, takes no initiative in goal-setting and sits waiting only for compensation information, the supervisor concludes that he or she doesn't care about doing the job well or improving. Respectful interaction during the appraisal reflects the quality of day-to-day work life. Setting aside sufficient uninterrupted time, in a private setting, is key. Confidentiality is, too. Only those with a need to know should be privy to the conversation or the form.

Don't prejudge. Our first impressions of others are automatic, largely unnoticed by our conscious minds. Past experiences, needs and wishes, and assumptions about the context in which we encounter new people all greatly influence what information we absorb and how we interpret it. Research indicates that even after months of regular interaction roughly two-thirds of our first impressions remain unchanged.[2] The hiring process alone does not give supervisors and employees the opportunity to know each other well, and upfront impressions can be frozen or misplaced without continuing, two-way feedback.

Keep messages clear and direct. Know when something needs to be said; then, based on solidly documented examples, be sure you relay it accurately. Never assume that supervisors or employees know what you think, want, or need. Not being direct can be costly. Hints are often misinterpreted or ignored. Keeping messages clear depends on awareness, knowing what you have observed, and knowing how you have reacted to it, especially since what we see and hear externally is so easily confused with what we think and feel inside. Separating these elements will go a long way toward communicating clearly and directly.[3]

A straight message is one in which the stated purpose is identical with the real purpose of communication. Disguised intentions and hidden agendas are manipulative. Check whether your messages are straight by asking:

- ✓ Why am I saying this to this person?
- ✓ Is this what I want him or her to hear, or something else?

You'll know quickly whether the points you're highlighting need to be clarified, strengthened or scrapped.

Review job description. Make sure there *is* a written job description and that it's accurate and up-to-date. If not, the supervisor should write one, with input from the employee, before the formal evaluation session so it can be discussed and used for the next review cycle. Along with goals, the job description is a key basis for gauging performance effectiveness and for ensuring that organizational and departmental needs, and supervisor and employee expectations, are on the same track. Perhaps new responsibilities have been added over the review cycle, or there's interest in adding them. There may be recent team or work group initiatives that should be integrated. Perhaps there is a community liaison role that has not been acknowledged. Employees are the people most aware of on-the-job responsibilities that are not in their job descriptions. Making sure they're included helps measure employee workloads and assess the need to develop new skills for performing new tasks.

Track performance year-round. Keep a folder handy to toss in quick notes as the year progresses—including positive observations, others' feedback, memos, award notices, e-mails, and other items that pertain to work performance. It's important to keep the folder active, not just one you dust off yearly. Use it as a basis for regular ongoing discussion. Doing this may seem time-consuming, but it's much easier, more productive, and more fair than having to draw on your memory once a year. An appraisal at the end of a work cycle works much better as a recap with recognition, or as an opportunity to stimulate improvement plans, than as a surprise that can make both supervisors and employees uncomfortable. Not having specific examples to support your ratings can lead to the legal problems noted in Chapter 8.

Stay up-to-date on organizational goals. Know what's going on in your organization. Effectively tying job description and goals to broader needs requires a good grasp of organizational direction and changes. Be prepared to factor what is newly needed and/or desired into ongoing responsibilities. When supervisors don't share information with staff, misinformation flies freely and morale can plummet. Employees should feel comfortable asking questions and offering to pitch in on new initiatives, even if supervisors seldom initiate discussion.

Consider the ground rules. If you're a supervisor, should there be ground rules for performance reviews? Does your organization mandate any? If not, perhaps it should. Ground rules might cover ensuring two-way conversation, setting guidelines for goal-setting and problem-solving, applying techniques to stay on track, developing standards for addressing conflict, and delaying talk about compensation for a timely follow-up session.

If you're an employee being appraised, the ground rules are more informal but nonetheless important—and up to you to implement. The most productive appraisals are clear, open two-way discussions. Honesty and clarity, bolstered by written examples, are fair expectations, but may require some added determination if your work climate does not readily invite openness.

Follow up promptly with compensation discussion. Thoughts about compensation inevitably shadow the appraisal session. That should come after the appraisal, whether or not during the same session. This precludes the tendency of employees to bring up examples of stellar performance and explain away anything that might take away from a raise. The meeting can turn into a battle of explanation and defense rather than an open discussion of performance and how it can be improved.[5]

Preparation Pays Off

Make sure to review:

- ✓ Your organization's strategic plan.
- ✓ Updated job description.
- ✓ Evaluation form/rating structure.
- ✓ Previous performance appraisal.
- ✓ Personnel file documentation.
- ✓ Goals for current review cycle.
- ✓ Preliminary appraisal recommendations—positive and/or negative aspects.
- ✓ Documented examples, including letters of praise and award information.
- ✓ As needed, suggestions for improvement, such as training, Performance Improvement Plan.
- ✓ List of questions.
- ✓ Anticipated reaction and how to best respond.

The Pre-Review

Before the review, employers sometimes ask staff to complete the actual appraisal form, or to perform self-evaluations and/or appraise their supervisors. Other forms may seek feedback about development needs, training interests, ideas for new projects, and areas of concern. The responses may be viewed in advance or discussed for the first time during the review. Many companies ask employees to be ready for the review meeting with a list of accomplishments. Even if not asked, it's an excellent idea to have one. It is also important that the supervisor's supervisor review the evaluation before it is shared with the employee. This provides built-in safeguards that can be significant to employees, supervisors, and organizations.

Documentation is key for both supervisors and employees. Not doing it year-round can backfire. In one case, a supervisor realized that her employee was not contributing the way he described it on his pre-appraisal form. She wanted to place him on probation, but without her own supporting documentation all she had to support doing so was his "on-the-record" account of stellar performance. It was only then that the supervisor began documenting his poor performance. Chapter 8 examines the legal importance of solid documentation.

Smart companies do everything they can to keep managers and employees comfortable with the performance appraisal. They underscore that it is part of the work process, and not an annual event. They circulate the appraisal form in advance so that features and ratings are clear. Many make it available on their Intranet. One association pulled together a panel of seasoned supervisors who talked about their own appraisal experiences and shared techniques that worked. Some organizations have a brown-bag lunch, show a video and encourage discussion.

At a country club in the mid-Atlantic, managers ask: "Will both the employee and I know when this goal has been achieved?" An international hotel chain develops appraisal forms designed to apply to particular jobs. A financial firm in Virginia has an optional employee pre-evaluation sheet that supervisors review before the evaluation and attach to the evaluation form. Five questions in the pre-review probe quality of performance against the performance plan, success in fostering customer satisfaction, team and work group contributions, challenges desired over the upcoming year, and the training needed to undertake them.

One company scheduled small group meetings so that supervisors who worked with certain employees could collectively share impressions of their work, giving more balance to each evaluation and fostering consistency in evaluations throughout the organization. Some organizations make sure that everyone—supervisors and employees alike—have copies of the firm's strategic plan in hand before the appraisal, with plenty of time to review it so that it dovetails with setting new goals. As a new evaluation cycle nears, some companies distribute articles to stimulate thinking about the process. Others pull together relevant "asset lists" of training possibilities, videos, and other resources. And a few organizations make sure that supervisors don't receive their reviews until all staff reviews are completed first.

To guide employees' preparation, it's helpful for supervisors to suggest they consider and answer three questions:[6]

- ✓ What actions have you taken?
- ✓ What discoveries have you made?
- ✓ What partnerships have you built?

Increasingly, smaller businesses, associations, law firms and other such organizations are recognizing the value of not only conducting performance reviews but also making sound preparation for them. Many conduct training sessions on conducting annual evaluation. Whether managed internally or handled by a consultant, the training takes many forms. It may be just for supervisors, or for both supervisors and employees in mixed or separate sessions. A labor lawyer, for example, might conduct training specific to legal issues. Role plays often provide useful coaching for both. Training workshops track the entire process, from broadly clarifying why appraisals are important, to self-assessment, goal-setting, problem-solving exercises, and being tuned in to rating errors.

New software is making record-keeping easier. Some products allow users to program in the strategic plan and goals. They also permit supervisors to type in employee ratings, yielding a clear, objective interpretation that helps them assess whether the rating really lines up with their intent. Seeing the write-up of a "poor rating," for example, may either bolster a supervisor's decision or trigger a change. The supervisor should add specific examples of work performance to document the rating.

The "A" List

As this book evolved, four specific elements of participation in successful evaluations—for both supervisors and employees—seemed constant among case studies, extensive research by others, and interviews of employees at all levels of various organizations: being **a**ctive, **a**ccurate, **a**ttentive and **a**ppreciative. These behaviors appear intrinsic in preparing for performance appraisals that foster excellent working relationships. All four can ease the communication between supervisors and employees year-round. While they are not the measurable standards on which performance reviews must be based, they are harbingers of positive on-the-job experiences and key aspects of effective supervisor/employee relationships.

Being active means sharing ownership of the evaluation. Active preparation, then enthusiastic engagement during the actual session, go a fair distance toward a supervisor's saying, "You matter," or an employee's communicating that "this work is important to me beyond a paycheck." Pride and accomplishment cannot be created outside of the job and work, but must grow out of them.[7] The performance appraisal is an excellent opportunity to wrap up a series of informal discussions, assess goals set during the previous cycle, and move forward in a way that builds pride, recognizes accomplishment, sets new goals and clarifies how needed corrections will be measured. As Will Rodgers put it, "even if you're on the right track, you'll get run over if you just sit there."[8] The performance review is what enables actively moving ahead.

Being accurate is a similarly indispensable dimension of performance appraisals. Documenting work performance is often challenging enough, even without opening the door to questions about accuracy. Because it's unreasonable to expect that all accomplishments, trip-ups, and other information important to the evaluation can be kept in sight throughout an entire cycle, particularly if it's a year long, there is a strong need for continual tracking. Recent accomplishments and initiatives will stay fresh, but accurately assessing the full scope of work during a cycle takes ongoing vigilance. Good records can mark the difference between "meeting" or "exceeding" expectations, or countering evidence that a performance is below par.

Being attentive means keeping your goals on the radar screen. It requires staying abreast of changing organizational needs and structure, new project opportunities, increased professional or personal stress, and other clues that can translate into changes in your work life. While not directly tied to performance appraisals, an understanding of such occurrences can help shape their outcome, especially if your attentiveness means initiating fresh responsibility, temporarily offering to pick up a project, or perhaps envisioning an added role for yourself or your department while organizational change is still in the planning stage.

Ideally, ***being appreciative*** wouldn't need to be built in, but it often does need to be. In whatever form, periodic recognition—from both sides of the desk—clearly eases the review process. Comments such as, "I knew what was coming would be fair," and "there are no hidden agendas" came from employees whose supervisors took the time to praise good work, explain any concerns, and simply thank their staff members for extra effort. Supervisors appreciated "questions in advance instead of missed deadlines when something isn't clear," "being trusted enough to be asked for support" and thanks for providing that support. "Employees increasingly believe that their job satisfaction depends on acknowledgment of work performance as well as on adequate salary."[9] Compensation in its many forms is examined in Chapter 5.

Three Scenarios

This book is really about human interaction. Throughout it, three composite characters based on actual people illustrate how that interaction occurs in the performance review process. Meet "Marilyn," "Richard," and "Peg":

Marilyn, 42, is office administrator of a medium-size law firm. She is constantly busy, with broad responsibilities for personnel, budget, new equipment, file indexes and occasional expansion of physical facilities. Marilyn is on the recruitment team for associate lawyers and coordinator of the annual attorney retreat. She is an excellent employee who manages her time well. She is well compensated and feels highly appreciated by both attorneys and support staff. Frequently approached by competing firms, Marilyn is a much-sought-after administrator. Her firm's challenge is to keep her satisfied and motivated.

To prepare for her performance appraisal, Marilyn can:

- ✓ Track her workload.
- ✓ Compare her present responsibilities with last year's job description, listing added responsibilities.
- ✓ List accomplishments during the current review cycle.
- ✓ Underscore how she leveraged those accomplishments.
- ✓ Envision what more she would like to do and describe any training she needs to do it.
- ✓ Draw on her excellent track record, clear value to her firm, and understanding of parameters to seek what she wants most.

Marilyn's supervisor can:

- ✓ Review her job description.
- ✓ Plan to recognize her terrific work, value to the firm, and continuing loyalty.
- ✓ Plan to acknowledge that she's in high demand.
- ✓ Set aside enough time to listen carefully and discuss her ideas and proposals thoroughly.
- ✓ Prepare new challenges to keep her motivated.

Richard, 36, is a supervisor in charge of overseeing the day-to-day operations of the duplicating department. He interviews and hires staff and ensures that they are well trained from the start. He assigns jobs to technicians, keeps tabs on new technology, verifies and approves time sheets, and makes sure that all duplicating requests are fulfilled quickly and efficiently. Richard used to excel on the job. Right now he's constantly distracted because one of his parents, who lives alone, is slowly recovering after a serious illness and needs his help. The organization's challenge is to support his present needs yet make sure that he returns to meeting his work responsibilities at an outstanding level.

To prepare for his performance appraisal, Richard can:

- ✓ Track his workload.
- ✓ Compare his present responsibilities with last year's job description.
- ✓ List added responsibilities.
- ✓ List any accomplishments he has achieved in the present review cycle.
- ✓ Prepare how to acknowledge his shortcomings at work that are a result of caring for his ill parent.
- ✓ Prepare a plan to help him deal with his added personal responsibility for what may become a long-term situation, while recommitting to focus more effectively at work.

Richard's supervisor can:

- ✓ Review job description.
- ✓ Prepare to acknowledge the difficult situation.
- ✓ Prepare a list of mounting concerns, but also some positives.
- ✓ Plan how to re-engage and refocus Richard, seeking his suggestions in advance so that the review, which Richard is probably dreading, will be more upbeat.
- ✓ Plan to set measurable goals for improvement, along with a time frame for assessing their achievement.
- ✓ Prepare information regarding the company's Employee Assistance Program and other resources that can help Richard.

Peg, 27, is the receptionist for an advertising agency. She greets clients, maintains security in the reception area, handles the switchboard, tracks comings and goings of employees, sets up client files, lines up equipment for meetings, and picks up secretaries' typing overloads. Peg is a poor performer. She is often late, takes unscheduled days off, does not consistently get deliveries out on time, and often errs in taking messages and other administrative duties. Despite several coaching sessions, some adjustment of her hours to accommodate travel time, monitoring to be sure her workload isn't excessive, and many reminders, Peg has shown little improvement. Her job is now in jeopardy, and her personnel file contains a written warning.

To prepare for her performance review, Peg can:

- ✓ Determine whether she values her job and wants to keep it.
- ✓ Review the warning in her personnel file, her job description, and her workload.
- ✓ Prepare a list of solutions to documented problems and propose deadlines for herself to implement them.

Peg's supervisor can:

- ✓ Review her job description.
- ✓ Review documented discussions and warnings.
- ✓ Document her performance since the most recent warning.
- ✓ Plan to express a continuing commitment to work with her and identifying training that can help improve her performance.

3

Appraisals That Don't Bite

Organizations...are not paying enough attention to doing the right thing, while paying too much attention to doing things right.

—Warren Bennis, presidential adviser
and leadership expert

Too often, the evaluation form becomes the centerpiece of the appraisal process, functioning as a hurdle to get over until the next deadline. A bank vice president reflected the thoughts of several interviewees: "Completing the form feels as if the appraisal is all done." Another manager said, "Evaluation forms leave lots of room for the negatives and just a few lines for the positive stuff." Perhaps this isn't surprising. "Many performance appraisals often seek out weaknesses rather than pointing out strengths [even though] individuals are employed for what they can do, not for what they cannot do."[1]

A survey of Fortune 500 companies showed that only about 10 percent of employees were satisfied with their organization's performance evaluation methods.[2] And, a survey by Harris Interactive/Taleo Performance Management reported that 57 percent of respondents had either never had a review or rated it from "neutral" to "not useful." A survey by Mercer Human Resource Consulting found that 78 percent of companies routinely conduct annual performance reviews and communicate the results to workers. But only 26 percent of employees said managers routinely provide constructive feedback and/or coaching.

What lost opportunities! Organizations invest millions in fostering motivated employees and many millions more to keep that motivation alive. Yet the performance appraisal is too seldom valued as a vital element of performance management.

Tapping Into Motivation

As J. Samuel Bois says in *The Art of Awareness*, "Motivation is what impels us to do certain things rather than others; to wish for certain things rather than others; to react to persons and situations in a manner peculiar to ourselves."[3] In other words, motivation is personal; the performance review must be too. Each review is a highly individual matter. What makes an employee want to excel? How can an employee best communicate his or her personal best to a supervisor? On either side of the table, tapping into motivation requires preparedness, understanding, sound listening skills and a supportive work climate. Above all, it requires a willingness to genuinely know the person you're facing. A review once a year won't do it. If performance feedback is not ongoing, the appraisal can happen almost by rote, reminiscent of how journalist Edwin Newman's wryly viewed the World Series, as "play determined not by the quality of the teams but by the annual occurrence of October."[4] With appraisals, both sides can emerge as winners.

Motivated individuals will seek that end. Abraham Maslow, an American psychologist, noted for his "hierarchy of human needs" helped explain that people, when not blocked, will move up a ladder of needs to fulfill their potential. Satisfying one need sets the stage for advancing to the next. In this chain of needs, Maslow placed "esteem" as fourth, before self-actualization, and after the satisfaction of physiological, safety, and social needs. He says, "Individuals are motivated by the esteem they hold for themselves and in which they are held by others. Although real achievements are rewards in themselves, there is much enjoyment from the recognition and respect of others."[5]

Published in 1959, the work of psychologist Frederick Hertzberg is often cited as empirical evidence supporting Maslow's needs' theory.[6] In focusing on reasons for job satisfaction and dissatisfaction, Herzberg, too, identified recognition as a factor in satisfaction. Among his principles for implementing job enrichment, Herzberg underscored "increased accountability, feedback and providing new learning experiences"[7] as fixtures of most sound performance reviews. Herzberg's research showed that linking work and personal satisfaction is a potent motivator.

If you're a supervisor headed into appraisal discussions, it's useful to remember that your best assets on the job go home at night. Successful change depends on individual people and their collective actions. As Norman R. Augustine writes, "By showing trust in and respect for all employees, managers can empower people to do their jobs to the very best of their abilities As Martin Marietta's former president, Tom Young, liked to observe, 'No one shows up in the morning thinking: I guess I'll see how badly I can mess up today, but an unenlightened management can put them in that frame of mind by 9 a.m.' By cultivating and investing time in employees, managers strengthen the foundation of the entire enterprise."[8]

As the employee being appraised, you might take inventory. Who you are determines what you see. Do you see a solution in every challenge, or a problem in every circumstance? When it comes to approaching problems, are you likely to flee them, fight them, forget them, or face them? It may be necessary to get out of the box of your typical thinking.[9]

Before the discussion, be very clear about what you value, what your supervisor or employee values, what your organization values, and the documentation vital to supporting these perspectives. Apply the four A's of positive-on-the-job experiences—being active, accurate, attentive, and appreciative (see Chapter 2)—and you're set to start the discussion.

Motivational Benchmarks

✓ Clear, challenging goals.
✓ Good working conditions.
✓ Reliable, helpful team members.
✓ Effective communication from above.
✓ Ongoing feedback from boss and others.
✓ Consistently applied policies and procedures.
✓ A certain amount of autonomy.
✓ Recognition for a job well done.

Upbeat Openings

In starting the discussion, supervisors might recall their own feelings about being evaluated. Empathy can spur an approach, tone, and even body language that makes the entire meeting less adversarial. Supervisors should realize that employees not only want feedback but have a right to it. Employees want to know how they're doing, whether expectations are on track, and what the future holds. They seek recognition and rewards. Supervisors want the satisfaction of a management function done well. If this discussion is the culmination of a series of two-way talks giving performance feedback, there should be no surprises. For example, one national financial institution uses a form that tracks goals throughout the entire performance cycle. Supervisors and employees meet at least quarterly, and both can gauge progress at any point along the way.

Usually evaluations are not so frequent, and sometimes it is helpful for the supervisor or employee to acknowledge up front that the appraisal discussion is a bit uncomfortable or anxiety-provoking. It provides the opening to reassure employees that the review contains many positive aspects. The supervisor can also underscore his or her interest in the employee's growth and development. Be clear that the goal is to summarize what has already been shared at mini-meetings and then to move on from there.

A brief warm-up can set a comfortable tone. While this is a professional meeting and small talk should be minimal, employees (and supervisors) must also be relaxed enough to become genuinely engaged. The aim is to be open, friendly, and positive. Both supervisors and employees can demonstrate interest in trading views and discussing particular projects or aspects of performance. The climate should be inviting and non-threatening, with both supervisors and employees open to hearing concerns without getting defensive. Supervisors might heed former U.S. Secretary of State Colin Powell's words: "The day soldiers stop bringing you their problems is the day you have stopped leading them."[10]

Employees need time to read and absorb what their supervisors have written. If they can't review the evaluation before the meeting, time to do so should be given early in the discussion. Supervisors may wish to step out of the office so employees can focus better. It's important for supervisors to reassure employees that the appraisal form is confidential and will not be left where others can read it.

Then, the supervisor and employee can review the appraisal form jointly and identify points of agreement or disagreement. If there is a self-appraisal, the supervisor and employee can go back and forth between the appraisal and self-appraisal forms throughout the meeting. Be ready to request (or provide) examples for any areas of disagreement.

Supervisors can kick off the discussion with such open-ended questions as:

- ✓ How do you think things have been going?
- ✓ Do my ratings seem fair? (If the answer is no) Why not?
- ✓ Is there anything that, with hindsight, you wish you'd done differently this year?

If an employee isn't ready or willing to participate, the supervisor can consider postponing the meeting, explaining that it won't be productive unless the employee actively participates. Emphasize that discussion is two-way. Considerable participation by and input from the employee is important for the employee's perception that the process is fair.[11] Setting expectations for the discussion up front can help.

Probing Questions

For Supervisors

✓ What do you think might help you meet next year's goals? What changes would you suggest?

✓ What would you like to work on?

✓ How can I best help you during the coming year?

For Employees

✓ How do you see my skills best fitting organizational needs?

✓ What's your reaction to [cite specific initiative]?

✓ What do you see as the next steps in my development?

✓ How can I better support you and this department?

✓ What do you see as my three key priorities in the months ahead?

Building Productive Discussions

A discussion involves two parties. They perform two equally important actions—*talking* and *listening*. One doesn't work well without the other. Other factors may also frame the appraisal discussion. The prior experiences or beliefs of one or both parties may play a part in how the conversation progresses. One of the parties may not be accustomed to discussing feelings beyond a narrow family circle. There may be concerns about rejection or punishment, or that revealing something positive will be perceived as bragging. There may also be fear of self-knowledge. We instinctively know that by disclosing ourselves, we come to know ourselves better.[12]

While shared feelings are the building blocks of a relationship, the most difficult part of communication may be that sharing itself. Some people don't want to hear what you feel. Some are selectively receptive. Yet how you feel is a large part of what makes you unique.[13]

Listening fully and openly is also a hallmark of productive evaluation sessions. Yogi Berra reportedly said, "You can observe a lot just by watching." The same applies to listening. There's a major difference between listening and hearing: listening is active; hearing is passive. Kicking off the appraisal discussion with open-ended questions will fall short if the other person is not actively listening. Absorbing the answers might contribute to a fairer rating. They might contain terrific ideas or clues flagging serious concerns. Vital bonds of shared understanding can be bolstered or flattened depending on the quality of listening.

Supervisors often build the appraisal discussion by reviewing significant accomplishments—giving praise and credit for quality work. When it's genuinely deserved, this praise is appreciated, and employees find it stimulating and motivating. Managers often begin with such statements as:

✓ *This year, you made important contributions in developing and administering our media strategies. On [dates], you were an effective spokesperson with the national and local press, and then on [date] you did an excellent job in explaining our initiatives to constituents.*

✓ *The research you carried out this year was impressive. You developed an effective research design and strategies for data collection and analyses. Because of your work, we'll be developing two new products.*

✓ *You've been more conscientious this year about managing the pension plan, processing 20 applicant loans, and preparing 11 reports and other information for the IRS audit.*

Supervisors generally work their way through each section of the form, focusing on technical aspects, then interpersonal ones. Objective measures are combined with soft skills. "What" was done and "how" the employee did it cover both bases. Statements and, as applicable, ratings should be documented by real work examples.

Active Listening

Aristotle counseled that we should use our two ears and one mouth proportionately. That's an important skill to practice if we're committed to listening actively rather than merely hearing. Wendi Eldh, a corporate trainer in Virginia, refers to active listening as a contact sport. She developed the following guidelines for getting it right:

- ✓ Be prepared to listen. Handle possible distractions before the conversation begins. Turn off cell phones and pagers.

- ✓ Focus on the speaker's words and body language. This requires turning off internal distractions, too. Without staring, try to absorb the full message—it's physical, emotional, and verbal.

- ✓ Consider your own body language. Does it indicate your level of listening? Is your level of openness in tune with the speaker's? The speaker may be watching for physical clues that you are listening, especially if his or her body language is open. A muted and closed expression or posture may convey your disapproval or disagreement.

- ✓ Open body language can include eye contact; relaxed, open arms; alert, upright posture; and nods affirming certain points. Closed body language might include folded arms, slumped posture, or shoulders or legs turned away.

- ✓ Provide verbal cues that you are being attentive. Periodically say, "yes," or "I see," or "I understand," to reinforce that you are listening. If you show a willingness to focus on distractions, you're not being attentive.

- ✓ Most importantly, use feedback and questions to clarify meaning. Paraphrase the speaker's message to be certain you have understood. This both reduces ambiguity and emphasizes that you are paying attention. This will also help you replace merely hearing with active listening and engagement.

Beyond the Comfort Zone

The following example shows how a supervisor addressed a problem, recognizing an employee's achievements yet candidly expressing, in a supportive way, exactly where improvement was required:

Doug, as project manager, you brought in that technology project on time and under budget. You used excellent planning and implementing skills. As we discussed when it happened, however, at times you weren't responsive when other task force members questioned a decision. At one point, you agreed to make a suggested change, but then you didn't talk to the team for the rest of the day.

You bring a number of good skills to your assignments. However, this organization also values true collaboration and teamwork. You need to interact with other team members consistently and in a way that makes them want to work on more projects with you. When team members make a suggestion, work with them to determine whether it would be useful. Express appreciation if it's an idea that will add value, or for just its suggestion, even if it wouldn't. And you should more actively elicit ideas from the group.

Why don't you think about building in a brainstorming session during the planning phase? That way, you empower the team, and you might get a quicker turn-around on the project. Working as a team is necessary for a "fit" here. I would be remiss if I didn't bring up this sensitive topic. You are an important member of the team, and I want you to be successful here.

I have more ideas about how you can work on this. Why don't you attend one of my task force meetings, so you'll be able to see what I mean in action.

After that, please let me hear your ideas for how you can work on this.

Feedback Sandwich

When feedback is especially tough and employees might react negatively, one HR manager advocates using a "feedback sandwich." Based on the understanding that "feedback" covers what one party needs, what the other party needs, and what the organization needs, the feedback sandwich is a six-step method for approaching a difficult discussion—with positive statements "sandwiching" the criticism.

- ✓ The supervisor opens the discussion with a positive aspect of the employee's performance.
- ✓ The problem is identified, and the supervisor explains his or her concerns.
- ✓ The employee is asked to explain his or her perspective.
- ✓ With examples, the supervisor outlines how the problem affects their organization's goals.
- ✓ The employee is asked for solutions, and the supervisor and employee together develop an action plan.
- ✓ The supervisor ends on an upbeat note, expressing confidence in the employee's ability to pursue a positive course.

Supervisors need to be direct about the behaviors they want to see. Employees should feel empowered to ask about their performance. Both should be open to a candid discussion designed to turn around below-par performance. In the previous example, if the supervisor hadn't suggested he build a brainstorming session and attend a task meeting to see how it's done, Doug could have walked away from his evaluation either thinking everything was great, or with the nagging feeling that he needed to improve but didn't know how.

Make appraisals constructive, specific and performance-focused, not personality-driven:

Vague	Specific
You are often late.	You arrived 15–30 minutes after the start of your shift four times this month.
You seem to make many errors.	During November, you made six errors on the monthly report, three errors on the customer letter, and routed five calls incorrectly.
You are never at your desk.	I went to your office four different times yesterday, and you weren't there.

Stay calm. Be encouraging. If you're the supervisor, never discuss the need for improvement harshly. Acknowledge any circumstances that were beyond the employee's control. Work for understanding rather than complete agreement. Aim to turn things around. Be ready to offer help. Clarify what needs to happen by identifying specific actions that the employee can take. Refer to resources you have identified before the meeting to give the employee direction; perhaps there's a helpful training class, a book, or mentor. Prepare a plan both of you can agree on. Most importantly, express confidence that you can work through the issues together. Continue to check for reactions and understanding throughout the discussion.

If you're the employee, be prepared with your own suggestions for improving your performance, and participate willingly in shaping a plan with clear benchmarks to mark your improved performance.

Targeting Objectives

The joint process of writing objectives clarifies and directs behavior, providing employees with results-oriented challenges. Involved employees share ownership and pride of outcome, rather than feeling as if objectives are being imposed on them. Whenever possible, build objectives around what employees most want to do. Motivated employees can make a pitch for the work they want, especially by underscoring organizational benefits. Objectives must be feasible within given time frames and include clear performance standards. Without performance standards, how can a supervisor and employee know that their objectives have been reached?

Performance standards work as yardsticks in measuring employee performance. In most cases, they measure either productivity or quality. A productivity standard would require a salesman to close ten sales in three months. A quality standard would require a salesman to close 10 sales in three months without any processing errors. When standards are clear and in writing, it's more difficult to disagree about whether a goal was met.

Employee-Driven Objectives

At the National Health Service Hospital in the United Kingdom, where supervisors and employees jointly set work objectives, employees reported finding the process beneficial as long as they were actively engaged in the process. They reported that the objectives they set for themselves were more interesting and challenging than those set by their supervisors. Employees also reported pursuing growth opportunities through the objective-setting process. Because the hospital encourages mini-reviews throughout the year, the annual reviews are mainly a confirmation of these agreements, allowing a focused look at objectives for the coming cycle.[14]

Sample measurement indicators include:[15]

1. Quantity
    ✓   Number of clients served per day.
    ✓   Number of items processed per week.
    ✓   Number of complaints handled per month.

2. Quality
   - ✓ Error rate/ratio.
   - ✓ Percentage of orders without errors.
   - ✓ Percentage of work redone.

3. Time
   - ✓ Number or percentage of deadlines missed.
   - ✓ Number of calls answered within three rings.
   - ✓ Turnaround time.

4. Cost
   - ✓ Percent of variance from budget.
   - ✓ Dollars saved over period.
   - ✓ Overtime.

Objectives can reflect basic job duties, special responsibilities for particular projects and organizational and departmental goals. Developmental areas for employees' growth are another important source of objectives. What can best help employee improve performance, move ahead or fulfill their particular interests tied to organizational needs? Discuss any obstacles, such as time constraints and availability of resources.

Successful Closes

As with the opening, aim for an upbeat close that paves the way for a mini-review in the near future. Before closing, supervisors can be sure that the job description is up to date. Employees can use this opportunity to suggest including newly desired challenges. For both supervisors and their employees, it's a good time to ask whether the current workload makes sense. As an employee, do you feel overwhelmed or underutilized? As a supervisor, do you know how your employees would answer?

Before closing, managers might invite feedback about their own performance. Asking what employees need from supervisors can yield a helpful blueprint for managerial efforts in the year ahead. As a supervisor, this blueprint could be handy during your own appraisal.

Objectives That Work

- ✓ Begin with an action verb.
- ✓ Specify, in writing, what needs to be accomplished.
- ✓ Clearly define how accomplishments are to be measured.
- ✓ Identify an end date.
- ✓ Link employee talents and organizational interests.

Example #1:

Design and conduct three supervisory-skills modules: the first by October 10; the second by January 10; the third by April 10. On the final test, everyone you have trained should achieve a score of 85 percent or higher. As the trainer, you should receive a 90 percent or higher approval rate from the participants on your delivery style and effectiveness.

Example #2:

Use various recruitment strategies to increase the number of 25- to 35-year-old members by 15 percent within the next three years. Recruitment strategies must include direct mail, community membership drives, Internet, electronic media, and local television and print media.

Summarizing what has been discussed is a productive way to close. To check for understanding, supervisors can ask employees to write the summary. Supervisors and employees might also share thoughts about what was learned, whether there were any surprises, whether the suggestions for improvement outweighed acknowledgement of accomplishments, and general reactions. Employees should know that the door is always open if they have a later reaction to anything in the appraisal. They can also respond in writing.

Close on a friendly note. Supervisors should reinforce that the employee is part of an important team and that his or her performance counts. They must make clear that the discussion is about business and the employee's place in this business. Employees should be appreciative of their supervisor's support and willingness to help guide their talents and interests, along with those of the organization. Appreciation must be expressed on both sides.

Employees sign and date the appraisal form with the understanding that this merely indicates that the form has been discussed. The employee should walk out with a copy of the form. Confidentiality can again be stressed. It's up to the supervisor to make sure any promised follow up occurs as quickly as is feasible. It's up to the employee to initiate feedback about any areas of particular concern, especially if the supervisor is likely to bring them up at the next mini review. It's also up to employees to keep supervisors informed about the work results of their effort to achieve the stated goals.

Weighing Objectives

Consider prioritizing objectives based on their importance. Supervisors and employees can do this together, factoring in:

✓ Impact on mission and strategic plan.
✓ Effort involved.
✓ Special knowledge or creativity required.
✓ Scope of project.
✓ Effect on other work.
✓ Repercussion of not achieving the objective.

Agree on a plan and commit it to paper. Make clear that the employee will be accountable for following through, and that the supervisor will monitor progress, provide guidance and be available for occasional collaboration.

Three Scenarios

Markedly different objectives highlight the appraisals of Marilyn, Richard, and Peg, the composite people introduced in Chapter 2. Because Marilyn is already a terrific achiever, the challenge for her evaluating supervisor is to keep her enthusiasm high and engage her in identifying fresh goals to pursue in the year ahead. Recognizing how she enjoys developing programs and administering details, Marilyn's supervisor acknowledges her value to the firm, then suggests she take on the planning for her law firm's legal and community activities over the coming year. Marilyn is asked to survey the firm's partners about topic choices, draft an agenda, suggest speakers, and present options and a budget to the planning committee within ten weeks. Her already considerable day-to-day responsibilities of keeping the law firm running smoothly are also updated and spelled out on her appraisal, each with measurable goals. Given her enthusiastic approach to implementing numerous tasks, Marilyn and her supervisor schedule a mini review in four weeks to be sure she's not too overloaded to meet expected deadlines.

Richard's situation is much different. Distracted by a serious family illness, he's a good worker whose performance is sliding. The challenge is to prevent further sliding and help renew Richard's pride in performing well. During the appraisal discussion, Richard's supervisor can acknowledge the difficulty of the situation and pass along the Employee Assistance Program information she obtained for him while preparing for the review. Because of Richard's excellent contributions to developing his company's Winter Technical Exhibit three years before, his supervisor works to engage him in the upcoming exhibit, not asking him to leave home to attend but, instead, partially delegating the responsibility of determining which of four senior copy technicians will represent their company. This will involve objectively discussing the qualifications of each technician with their respective supervisors as part of the exhibit planning team, contributing to a written report, and helping to prepare the designated technician to attend, including providing input for a panel discussion and computer demonstration. This work all needs to be effectively concluded by the exhibit's opening in two months. Goals for Richard's daily responsibilities are set as well. The supervisor closes by acknowledging the tough circumstances and reinforcing that she has full confidence in Richard's commitment to meet his responsibilities. A mini review is scheduled in three weeks to monitor his work.

Despite continuing support, Peg's performance continues to be poor. But rather than turn the appraisal session into a termination, her supervisor again explains the concerns about Peg's performance and its adverse impact on the organization. The supervisor also tries to have Peg acknowledge her behavior. As a last effort to find a solution, the supervisor wants to schedule a meeting the following week to discuss a plan to quantify her improvement. Peg agrees, realizing this is her last chance to keep her job.

Types of Appraisals

Performance reviews can be recorded in many forms and by various methods.

Absolute Standard or Category Rating

This is a single-form recording method.

- ✓ **Adjective Rating Scale:** Also known as the Graphic Scale Appraisal, this is one of the oldest and most popular methods. As the chart below shows, the appraiser marks the rating that best describes the employee's performance. Generally, there is a "comments" section for specific examples to support the rating.

Performance Factor	Performance Rating
Initiative: Willingly assumes new and challenging assignments. Is self-directed and motivated. Anticipates what needs to be done and does it.	_____ Far exceeds expectations
	_____ Exceeds expectations
	_____ Meets expectations
	_____ Partially meets expectations
	_____ Does not meet expectations

- ✓ **Checklist Appraisal:** On this form, the supervisor responds to the list of behavioral descriptions. Sometimes items are weighted to reflect importance.

Does the HR assistant:	Yes	No
1. Post job ads on time?	❏	❏
2. Prepare complete orientation packets?	❏	❏
3. Maintain files accurately?	❏	❏
4. Answer employee questions promptly?	❏	❏
5. Computerize data promptly?	❏	❏
6. Support other staff as requested?	❏	❏

✓ **Forced-Choice Appraisal:** Choosing between two or more specific statements, the supervisor selects one that best describes the employee. In a variation of this form, the appraiser selects a statement that is "most like" the employee and another that is "least like."

Relative Standards or Comparative Ratings

These methods compare employees against other employees.

✓ **Group Order Ranking:** Using this method, the supervisor ranks all employees who report to him or her so as to extract a particular classification, such as the top third.

✓ **Individual Ranking:** Employees are ranked according to their work performance, from highest to lowest. There can be no ties.

✓ **Paired Comparison:** Comparing each employee with every other member of the group, this method ranks employees' performance by counting the number of times any individual is rated the highest within the group.

Narratives

These take the form of a written assessment as opposed to a checklist.

✓ **Essay Appraisal:** The essay, which can be whatever length the supervisor desires, describes employee strengths, areas for development, achievement of goals, plans for improvement or development, and so forth.

✓ **Critical Incident Appraisal:** Focusing on key behaviors that define aspects of the job, the supervisor writes specific, work-related anecdotes conveying what an employee did or didn't do.

Behaviorally Anchored Rating Scales

Coupling elements from the Critical Incident Appraisal and the Adjective Rating Scale, the supervisor rates employees' performance of specific tasks, using a continuum from low to high, for example, from 1 to 5.

Employee Feedback Form

Is employee feedback built into your organization's evaluation form? If not, you may wish to check the feasibility of including a form for it in your appraisal process. Perhaps you can pilot it in your own department; then, if you're pleased with the results, suggest it be used organization-wide. The idea is to generate thinking from employees that will be helpful during the appraisal discussion, or as part of a mini-review. Just as important, it conveys the message that employee input counts. This form complements the probing questions on page 38:

Here are five questions that can help jump-start our appraisal discussion on [date]. Responding is voluntary, but I hope you'll think about responses and jot down your thoughts so we can discuss them during our meeting, to make sure we're both clear about how your work can be as gratifying as possible.

✓ *What work do you most enjoy doing? Are there a few areas that stand out?*

✓ *What responsibilities brought you the most satisfaction during the past [length of review cycle]?*

✓ *Ideally, what would you like to do that you're not doing now?*

✓ *What would it take to do this? How can I help you?*

✓ *Can I help you in other aspects of your work?*

4

Mission: Possible

Teamwork is the ability to work together toward a common vision, the ability to direct individual accomplishment toward organizational objectives. It is the fuel that allows common people to attain uncommon results.

—Andrew Carnegie, industrialist, businessman, philanthropist

Every successful organization has a mission, a vision of its own reason for being and its future. Think of it as the umbrella goal toward which everyone, from the CEO to the receptionist, is working together. How do you ignite that mission on all levels of the organization? How do you keep the vision glowing as it's translated into goals, objectives and performance measures, tied up in budgets, and bounced about in often uncertain economies?

The motivation begins at the top. "Producing change is about 80-percent leadership—establishing direction, aligning, motivating and inspiring people—and about 20-percent management—planning, budgeting, organizing and problem-solving," writes Harvard professor John Kotter. But leadership "exists at all levels of an organization. At the edges of the enterprise, leaders are accountable for less territory. Their vision may sound more basic; the number of people to motivate may be two. But they perform the same leadership role as their senior counterparts. They excel at seeing things through fresh eyes."[1]

Top CEOs understand this. UPS's cofounder and former CEO, James Casey, is credited with not just pioneering a company but building a culture. Yet he once admonished a reporter to, "remember the story is to be about us—not about me. No single individual should be given a disproportionate share of the credit."[2] Similarly, Louis V. Gerstner dedicated his book *Who Says Elephants Can't Dance* to "the thousands of IBMers who never gave up on the company, their colleagues, and themselves. They are the real heroes of the reinvention of IBM."[3]

At a discussion in August 2001, Dr. Lionel Tiger, of Rutgers University, said, "Leaders often forget that people are predisposed to do a good job. I'm always impressed with the films in which the young player rushes up and says, 'Send me in, coach.' People are hardwired to want to be sent in. One of the things good leaders do is to allow people to do what is built into them to do anyway, which is to contribute."[4]

It's All About Values

But contribute what, and how? Suppose an employee is working really hard, doing his or her best, yet still not doing what is best for the organization. The reason for this outcome may be that the company's "core purpose" is not clear. In a Harvard Business discussion, it was said, "Core purpose reflects an organization's reason for being. An effective purpose reflects idealistic motivations for doing the company's work. It doesn't just describe an organization's output or target customers; it captures the soul of the organization."[5]

For this soul to reach every cubicle, it needs to be integrated through all aspects of work. It can't just be a slogan on the wall, or perks given out simply to say "good job," unless that job is performed so as to advance the organization's mission and the employee understands that he or she not only performed well but also furthered the company's core purpose. Trying to enlist employees in a "purpose" is futile if that purpose is not explicit in job descriptions, objectives, and performance measures. Supervisors and employees are bound to feel uncertain about their own value in an organization if the link between their work and organizational mission and values is not clear and in the forefront of every part of their work.

Core values are the essential and enduring tenets of an organization. A small set of timeless guiding principles, core values require no external justification; they have *intrinsic* value and importance to those inside the organization.

The Walt Disney Company's core values of imagination and wholesomeness stem not from market requirements but from the founder's belief that these qualities should be nurtured for their own sake. William Procter and James Gamble instilled in P&G's culture a focus on product excellence, not merely as a strategy for success but almost as a religious tenet. Service to the customer is a way of life at Nordstrom that traces its roots back to 1901, eight decades before customer service programs became stylish. As former Johnson & Johnson CEO Ralph S. Larsen put it, "The core values embodied in our credo might be a competitive advantage. But that's not *why* we have them. We have them because they define for us what we stand for."[6] Such convictions are the spirited force that Peter Drucker described as "turning out energy larger than the sum of the efforts put in."[7]

Even with organizational principles firmly embedded, if awareness of them stays in the boardroom, most employees may not even know they exist. For this reason, communicating an organization's vision and strategy to every employee should be viewed as an internal marketing campaign. Its goals are identical to those of traditional marketing campaigns: to create awareness and affect behavior.[8]

Capturing the essence of core values and purpose is not an exercise in semantics. The point is not to create a perfect statement but to convey a deep understanding of your organization's core values and purpose, which can then be expressed in many ways. The idea is not to spout a slogan but to "get upfront and personal" with an organization's reason for being, to mainstream its principles and practice its values as a given of daily work life.

Georgia-Pacific's Cascading Goal-setting

Georgia-Pacific believes it's critical that an employee understand how what they work on every day directly links with and supports the organization's mission:

"Georgia-Pacific recognized that its processes for reviewing and managing performance were cumbersome and, more important, did not always provide a clear link between employee activities and the goals of the organization. To restructure its performance-management systems, the company designed a database, accessible to salaried management online and in real time, that defines a standard competency set applicable to all employees. The Georgia-Pacific strategic planning process generates company goals and measures that are set in January and then cascaded to all levels of the organization. The new performance management process then links these organizational objectives to individual performance targets, establishing a clear link between objectives and daily employee activities."[12]

Creating a sound link with organizational mission and strong recognition for workers contributing to it can become even more crucial in a down economy. Mary Hayes wrote in *Information Week* that "in tough times, companies are seeing the value of making sure employee goals are closely aligned with the goals of the business overall."[9] Computer software, carefully tailored to mission and values, or goal-alignment software, can help employees develop goals, as well as tracking reviews, bonuses, and merit pay increases. Analyst Maria Schafer emphasizes that how the tracking is explained is all-important: "If you say, 'We're going to be tracking you and watching you,' who wants that?" Instead, she says, companies must show employees that they're stakeholders in the business and that the more insight they have into corporate strategies, the more likely their company's success.[10]

NationsBank, now integrated with Bank of America, has used goal-alignment software effectively. Its software gathers relevant information from every organizational level and transmits it to executives as brief electronic reports. If executives want more detail about a given performance measure, they can double-click the item in the electronic report."As a result, managers at every level can readily see if targeted objectives are being met, can tell where the best performance is coming from, and reward those responsible," wrote Omar Aguilar in an article for *Strategic Finance*.[11]

Doing Your Best vs. Doing What's Best for Your Company

A vision provides the focal point, but, to manage performance effectively, employee performance must be aligned with organizational goals. As Peter Drucker wrote, "The real difficulty lies not in determining what objectives we need, but in deciding how to set them."[13] In other words, "how can both managers' and their boss' eyes be focused on what the job—rather than the boss—demands?"[14]

In *The Art of Awareness,* J. Samuel Bois wrote that communication is a vital start: "It's a two-way affair, and the receiver's function is no less important than that of the sender."[15] Regardless of whether everyone "buys in" to the organization's goals, each person in an organization can be expected to understand them. And buy-in tends to grow as employees feel connected to a mission, understand why and how their contributions are significant, and have performance measures directly linking their specific contributions to organizational goals.

The performance appraisal, as a mainstreamed asset, can help drive the entire organization toward a shared vision that reflects proudly on everyone in the organization. "A team isn't really a team if it isn't going anywhere," wrote John C. Maxwell in *The 17 Essential Qualities of a Team Player.* "And if the values, mission, goals and practices of a team don't match up, you're going to have a tough time as a team player."[16]

Supervisors and other managers should be evaluated on how well their departments contribute to accomplishing strategic goals. To get everyone on board, accountability needs to cascade from the top. One human resources consultant, called in to train 180 supervisors on applying strategic goals to individual departments, learned quickly that the supervisors had no idea what these new goals were; they had not been shared—on any level—prior to the training.

Even supervisors who are well grounded in goals can be helped by being trained to not just implement, but also to identify and frame goals. If "improve customer service by 30 percent" is a priority, every department in the organization should spell out what, how, over what time frame, and at what cost it plans to effect the goal. Each department can contribute, even if its function isn't to provide customer service directly. The point is that everyone works together.

Goal-directed performance appraisals might be viewed as a six-step process:

1. Establish business objectives and strategic goals.
2. Effectively communicate business objectives and goals.
3. Assess organizational structure's alignment with business objectives and goals.
4. Assess the employee's capacity to achieve business objectives and goals.
5. Fill in the gaps between capacity and business objectives and goals.
6. Implement, measure, and modify goals.[17]

When properly executed, an appraisal can become a powerful tool for establishing corporate culture and ensuring that employees understand and act on the organization's broad strategic goals.

Management by Objectives

An evaluation strategy called Management by Objective (MBO) encourages a supervisor/subordinate partnership that looks ahead. The focus is on goals to be achieved, rather than on past performance. The staff person, actively engaged in the process, is responsible for managing his or her own job performance, rather than just getting "marked" on what has already occurred.

Popular in private and public organizations,[19] the original MBO concept came from the accounting firm of Booz, Allen, and Hamilton and was called a "manager's letter." The process consisted of having all the subordinate managers write a letter to their superiors detailing what their performance goals were for the coming year and how they planned to achieve them.

Beyond an evaluation program or process, MBO reflects an "entire philosophy of management practice, a method by which managers and subordinates plan, organize, control, communicate, and debate. By setting objectives through participation, or by assignments from a superior, the subordinate is provided with a course to follow and a target to shoot for while performing the job."[20] Goals are objective, often quantifiable, and almost always in writing.

Strategic Human Resources

Top management might begin to look toward the human resources department as less of a "service only" department and more of a strategic unit, like marketing. Why not invite the head of human resources to participate in the strategic planning process? He or she can provide ideas on how to use performance appraisal as a tool for attaining organizational goals. Don't stop at goal-setting. Craft a full plan that periodically measures effectiveness, rewards advances, and derails failure. Organizational vision is the framework in which all employees are expected to measure up, knowing they can count on informed, enthusiastic support along the way. Discussing vision's role in running an organization, Merck & Company former Chairman and CEO Raymond Gilmartin said, "Everything you do is for a reason, and that reason is contained within the vision."[18]

Because this approach is built on specific goals, it is critical that these goals be aligned with organizational vision and priorities, not only across a company, but within a department. Given their prominence, these are the goals that a staff person will feel most responsible for achieving.

MBO works something like this:

✓ Employee creates a goal list (not too long), or the employee and supervisor develop it together—goals are concrete, realistic, and challenging, and they include time lines.

✓ Goals are considered in the context of organizational mission and needs of and department needs, along with the employee's talents and interests, including training or other support needed to address the goals.

✓ The goals may be modified as needed; then the employee and supervisor agree on a written list of specific goals.

✓ The two develop a clear action plan.

✓ Throughout the evaluation cycle, the supervisor informally encourages goal attainment, and the employee takes the initiative to check in.

✓ At the end of the evaluation cycle, they meet to discuss outcomes and repeat the process for the upcoming cycle, possibly retaining some goals that have not yet been fully achieved.

Three Scenarios

Here's how the performance reviews of Marilyn, Richard, and Peg are linked to the goals of their organizations:

Marilyn's law firm has set a goal of 15-percent revenue growth over the next 12 months and will hire seven associates to reach that goal. Because Marilyn coordinates new hires in her role as office administrator, she and the managing partner identified nine new objectives. Several of them give Marilyn new challenges and involve some traveling, which she has been eager to do:

- ✓ Participate in on-campus recruiting at five law schools.
- ✓ Select attorneys who will conduct on-site interviews.
- ✓ Be sure all travel and related arrangements are made.
- ✓ Circulate the resumes of screened candidates.
- ✓ Create schedules for students to be interviewed at the firm.
- ✓ Distribute and explain the interview assessment form.
- ✓ Collect completed assessment forms, tally them, and present the results to the managing partner.
- ✓ Ensure that follow-up letters are sent to every candidate interviewed.
- ✓ Coordinate final hiring details as requested by managing partner.

Richard, in his supervisory role, understands that his company must produce cutting-edge products to meet customer needs and stay competitive. Therefore, he is expected to continually learn all he can and stay on top of new developments. Given the situation with his ill parent, he has not pursued new training during the past several months. Loss of a recent order made the lapse even more apparent.

To meet organizational revenue goals, he worked out the following objectives with his supervisor; each advances organizational goals, yet are attainable despite Richard's need to spend time with his parent. Over the next four months, Richard will be evaluated on four new objectives:

- ✓ Identify and participate in two to four short-term training courses, some of which may be available online or during work time rather than as evening or Saturday seminars.
- ✓ Identify four to seven potential new customers and work with his supervisor to set up a two-hour training session demonstrating their company's newest capabilities.
- ✓ Follow up by phone with participants and assess their level of interest, submitting a report to his supervisor.
- ✓ Meet with the supervisor in four months to discuss how well he has met these objectives.

As for Peg, given her continuing poor performance record, her supervisor sits down with her and asks how Peg thinks she can be more helpful at their advertising agency. The question has an upbeat tone. It also puts more responsibility on Peg, making her accountable for a workload that she helps shape. If Peg really doesn't want to begin contributing to the agency at an acceptable level, it will be clear.

The discussion generates three objectives that, along with already assigned tasks, will drive Peg's performance. A follow-up discussion is scheduled in three weeks to review only these new objectives, each of which is geared toward strengthening customer service, designed to help generate new business. A discussion is scheduled in six weeks to review Peg's progress toward all her objectives. The new objectives include:

- ✓ Greet clients by name and ensure that their requests are met within one day, alerting a supervisor if that is not feasible.
- ✓ Attend the weekly staff meeting, select one project that is discussed, and suggest a way she can contribute to it. Ensure that the front desk is covered during the hour-long meeting, coordinating with a supervisor to secure the designee's commitment two days in advance.
- ✓ Offer to help out at next week's exhibit showcasing campaigns developed for the agency's clients during the past year, again coordinating with a supervisor so that the front desk will be covered.

5

The Many Facets of Compensation

Not everything that can be counted counts, and not everything that counts can be counted.

—Albert Einstein, Nobel Prize–winning physicist

Defined in its broadest sense, compensation is any reward or payment given for services performed. Operationally, that definition tends to narrow according to the definer's perspective. Managers typically define compensation as the financial rewards package provided to employees in exchange for their services—wages, salaries, commissions, and bonuses, plus insurance and other types of indirect monetary benefits. Employees generally think of compensation more narrowly, as the wage or salary they receive from their employers for their work.[1]

The difference is not subtle. With 30 percent or more of compensation in benefits, most employees are receiving significantly more than the bottom line, or net pay, on the check they take home. It's not unusual for employees to be happily surprised when their benefits are quantified—not just as numbers in paychecks that may not be scrutinized regularly, but as a concrete breakdown that is flagged during the compensation discussion phase of the performance appraisal.

As explained in *Managing Compensation (and Understanding It Too)*, "The *total* rewards package has three purposes:

1. To **attract** a sufficient number of qualified workers to fill organizational positions.

2. To **retain** employees so that turnover is held to acceptable levels.

3. To **motivate** employees to perform to the fullest extent of their capabilities."[2]

Organizational rewards packages are usually structured with three main components:[3]

1. **Direct Monetary Rewards.** Sometimes called cash compensation, direct rewards include everything (such as salary, wages, commission) that an employee is paid for work accomplished or effort expended. This income is discretionary.

2. **Indirect Monetary Payments.** Usually called benefits, these payments include items of financial value that do not result directly in employees' receiving spendable dollars. They cover various forms of protection, such as health, life, and disability insurance, and services, such as uniforms, free parking, financial counseling, and employer subsidized cafeterias.

3. **Psychological Satisfactions.** Psychological benefits are key in work environments. This type of compensation includes recognition, opportunities to perform meaningful work, social interaction, job training, advancement possibilities, and similar factors.

There are two fundamental compensation philosophies:

1. The **entitlement philosophy** is often characterized by cost-of-living raises and across-the-board pay increases. Eligibility is longevity-based. There is either a general pay increase for all employees, the same increase for

all employees within a classification, or a step increase within a pay grade or range.[4] While the performance appraisal is crucial for feedback, development, and other purposes, it provides little, if any, assistance when pay is entitlement-based.

2. The **performance-based philosophy** entails a variable pay approach, in which pay increases or decreases based on a measure of performance. Not everyone in the same job will be paid exactly the same, and not everyone will like the approach.[5] By documenting performance that can support or discourage a pay increase, performance appraisals are usually a vital aspect of performance-based compensation.

Communicating About Pay: Shadowing the Appraisal

The discussion about pay is usually more effective when held apart from the performance evaluation. If not kept apart, talk about compensation can be distracting. Mentioned upfront, an employee may be mentally computing the new amount, or feeling down because it's less than anticipated. If kept to the end, the employee may wait tensely for the figure and fail to actively engage in the appraisal discussion. Either way, talk about pay might affect the entire discussion.

Pay, however, does shadow most formal evaluations. Employees will be eager to find out about future paychecks, and supervisors will either want to recognize good work with a tangible reward or perhaps just get past disappointing news (although there is ample feedback that shows they are more likely to delay the discussion than to quickly get through it). But pay is inextricably tied to appraisals, and it's fair for employees to expect that the compensation will be scheduled at the end of the appraisal meeting, or soon after.

At the meeting, the supervisor should be prepared to thoroughly explain why and *how* the salary decision was made, not just in the context of the employee's performance but in line with overall compensation decisions. If an employee would have received more in better economic times, he or she has the right to know it. If there is a tight pool and others have performed more effectively, that should be communicated honestly as well. The supervisor needs to clarify what the raise is based on, the range of possible increase amounts, and the reasoning that supports the sum awarded.

If supervisors have stayed on top of appraisals through a series of mini-discussions, and employees have stayed actively engaged, the discussion about money should include no real surprises. If there are surprises, supervisors might question whether they said anything misleading, and employees might question whether there are real lags in their performance and, if so, what it will take to correct them.

Talking About Dollars

The best of supervisor/employee relationships can get sticky when it comes to compensation. This is especially true when a tight financial pool must be distributed among several highly deserving team members. Here's a look at how Mark (employee) and Carol (supervisor) candidly address his justifiable request for a financial reward and her justifiable need to dole out limited dollars fairly. Both hold their ground, yet engage in a respectful give-and-take as Mark's performance appraisal comes to a close:

Carol: Mark, I looked over the contributions you made recently, and I'm so pleased. The coordination you handled and the research you applied to our new series of public seminars are terrific. You really helped the department by designing and conducting that needs assessment. The new products were just what our customers wanted. You were critical to the launch of those products, too. And as a result of your outreach and creative client communications, this year's first five product seminars were filled to capacity. I don't know who worked harder on them than you.

Mark: Thanks for noticing all that. I spent a lot of time on those efforts and think my input really helped.

Carol: *I'll make sure you get a copy of this appraisal. As you've just seen, your contributions are highlighted in the summary section. And I'll definitely be thinking about another opportunity for you to use your creativity and perseverance.*

[Carol stands up to close discussion]

Mark: *I'd like to discuss one more point with you. Didn't you just tell me I worked harder than anyone else? And that my efforts resulted in some real success for us, some additional revenue?*

Carol: *Yes. I also put that in writing on the appraisal form.*

Mark: *Well, this is a little awkward, but I feel I merit something more for all of the extra time I put in. I spent five complete weekends in a row working on this project, and also many late evenings. I brought in 25 new customers this quarter and worked on the committee to design an online customer order form. There have already been more than 1,000 hits on it.*

Carol: *We'll be talking about increases at another meeting, Mark. This one is just to assess your performance, which is excellent. But I do want you to know that I don't have a lot of flexibility with increase amounts. I have to spread a finite amount among all six of you on my team. I'm not at liberty to discuss your coworkers, but I value each of you for your unique strengths.*

Mark: *But you said I worked harder than anyone.*

Carol: *I recognized you for your efforts, but please understand that other members of the team have done a series of similar projects—most have also been successful and generated additional revenue. What I plan to do is distribute the increases in an equitable way. I do have access to a small discretionary fund that I use for one-time bonuses. I'm glad you pointed out those additional contributions. I plan to look at all the data and make those awards next week. I promise you'll know something soon.*

Mark: *I hope all of my work will count.*

Carol: *I won't forget you, Mark. Your work is excellent, and I appreciate it. But until I take a comprehensive look at our budget and figure out a fair increase distribution across the board for all the employees, I cannot commit to anything. Thank you for being patient.*

What Counts?

Employees aren't the only ones appraised by their companies. Jobs themselves undergo a process of evaluation and analysis, in part to help establish a pay structure. "Job evaluation" is the process of analyzing and ranking all the jobs in a given organization to determine the value of each job in relation to the others. Organizations generally use one of these methods:

- ✓ **Classification Method.** Pioneered by the federal government, this approach seeks to identify common skill sets, expertise, or responsibilities across a wide range of different job descriptions. A supervisor with an MBA who manages 10 to 20 employees would be classified with a similar supervisor elsewhere in the organization, even if one were working in manufacturing and the other in marketing.

- ✓ **Ordering Method.** Sometimes called the "ranking method," this approach is much more subjective. A special committee, usually comprising both management and employee representatives, hammers out the relative rank of each job in the company without using specific weighting criteria. The committee simply asks, "Which is more important to us—Job A or Job B?" This method works well for small organizations, but it can be very difficult to administrate in companies with hundreds of positions.

- ✓ **Point Method.** This is perhaps the most objective (but also the most complicated) of the three approaches. In this method, management assigns a point value to each of the skills, education levels, or other requirements necessary to do a given job. The job of nuclear engineer, for example, might be assigned many more education points than that of file clerk. Add up all the points, and the organization has objective criteria for comparing jobs and establishing pay structures. It takes a lot of work to put a point system in place, but afterwards the organization has a fair, reliable, and objective system that can work for years.

It's Not Just About Pay

Pay has substantive and symbolic components. In signaling what and who in the organization is valued, pay both reflects and determines the organization's culture. Therefore, managers must be sure that pay practices send the company's intended messages. Talking about teamwork and cooperation and then not having a group-based component to the pay system matters, because paying solely on an individual basis signals what the organization believes is actually important—individual behavior and performance. Talking about the importance of all people in the organization and then paying some disproportionately more than others belies that message.[6]

Performance appraisals send powerful messages about an organization's principles. The care with which evaluations are developed, *whether* they are developed, and how timely and tailored they are, convey how much the company values its employees. And the extent to which employees participate in the process reflects their commitment, as well. Given that appraisals themselves can be awkward and "pay is a difficult topic of conversation in most organizations…altogether taboo in many workplaces [and] simply not discussed unless absolutely necessary,"[7] the coupling of a genuine talk about evaluation and pay may be a conversation still waiting to happen. How pay is structured and the thoroughness with which a manager addresses it "reflect a fundamental [organizational] belief about people, motivation, and management."[8]

But it's important to have this conversation. Having an attractive benefits package is not enough. Employees must have ample knowledge of all benefits available and the value of those benefits. Yet research has indicated that the typical employee is able to recall less than 15 percent of the benefits received from the company. Effective communication is apparently the exception rather than the rule.[9]

This is unfortunate because, beyond the "how much," employees care about understanding the "why" of their pay. "While the actual amount is very important, they want to know the rationale behind it. Research has shown that pay satisfaction increases with understanding of the pay scheme."[10]

Employees must see rewards as fair and equitable in order to be motivated. Equity theory emphasizes that an individual is concerned not only with the absolute rewards for efforts contributed, but also, and perhaps more important, with the relationship of his or her rewards and efforts to the rewards and efforts of others.[11] Employees' comfort levels with compensation and recognition for work performed will also help shape other factors, such as turnover and absence, all of which are directly linked to over-all organizational morale, productivity, and competitiveness.

By developing a keen understanding of organizational compensation policy, and amplifying that knowledge with specifics linked to individual employees, managers have an opportunity to build trust and strengthen communication in an area that is often difficult. They can be terrific ambassadors in showcasing company benefits and organizational values.

Communicating About Pay

There are several things to keep in mind when delivering news about pay.

Specificity Is Key

A manager's promise of a "good increase" may not look so good to an employee. A remark such as, "I'm going to get you the most I can," may build unrealistic expectations. "It is important to work out the details beforehand so that specifics can be clearly communicated...," writes Terry Satterfield in "Speaking of Pay," an article in HR magazine. "No chance of misunderstanding or false expectations can be permitted."

Pay Is Relative

"Each individual has a unique set of personal circumstances that make a given number high or low...same for the company," writes Satterfield. Supervisors should understand the "reference point," the factors such as performance, market, and economy that go into compensation, and explain them. Explaining can mean the difference between a disappointed, frustrated employee and a disappointed employee who appreciates being told about the bigger picture—and sees it.

All Pay Is Not Created Equal

Base pay and bonuses, the most common forms of direct cash compensation, require different discussions. Talk about base pay is more general and balanced. Market practices, budget realities, and pay range are reference points. Bonuses offer a terrific motivational opportunity. "Handing money to an employee while discussing actions and behaviors [you] would like to see repeated creates a powerful link between performance and reward," writes Satterfield.[12]

Ways to Pay

- ✓ **People-Based Pay.** The bureaucratic job-based approach used to determine pay won't be the major format driving pay system designs of the 21st century. Instead, the new designs will be people-based, driven by today's service and knowledge sectors.[13]

- ✓ **Skill-Based Pay.** Master new skills and boost earnings. No one receives a raise or promotion until new proficiency is demonstrated. Instead of job descriptions, "person" and "skill block" descriptions are developed. The evaluation tools include direct observation, testing, and measurement of results.

- ✓ **Knowledge-Based Pay.** Be rewarded for acquiring additional knowledge, performing either the current job or a new one.

- ✓ **Credential-Based Pay.** Be recognized for having a license or diploma, or passing examinations given by a third party professional or a regulatory agency.

- ✓ **Feedback Pay.** Job descriptions become mission statements aligned with strategic business objectives that establish a direct link between an employee's role and accomplishing those objectives.

- ✓ **Competency-Based Pay.** Subjective measures, which now are not usually considered, are added to skills, knowledge, and credentials. Motives, values, self-image, and even social role might be included. It's difficult to assign a dollar value on this model.

Pay for Performance

Pay for performance describes a broad range of pay practices. Repeated raises, while not meant as such, might be considered entitlements if they are not linked to specific performance achievement. Pay for performance is intended to link a worker's actions to his or her well-documented level of performance. Despite the commitment of management time and administrative complexity required, nearly one out of six organizations use such systems.[14]

Just like the appraisals they're often tied to, salary structures have changed through time. The traditional structure is hierarchical, with minimum to maximum ranges and grades and narrow pay bands. There may be a few dozen such ranges. This structure often supports traditional **merit pay** programs driven by appraisal systems that yield overall numerical scores. Perceived as being more objective than other structures, the traditional one is often an integral part of an organization's management style.[15]

Base pay, also a traditional form of compensation, provides direct compensation not affected by weekly productivity. However, the performance appraisal system and a job market study of average pay rates is crucial in justifying and determining an increase in base pay.[16]

Skill-based pay focuses on the fundamental knowledge, skills, and abilities required of a position. But developing the performance criteria for assessing a skill can be very time consuming, and the skills may become outmoded, replaced by technological developments. And then what is to be done with the worker? Reduce his or her pay given the obsolete skills? Raise the worker's pay for achieving the replacement skills?[17]

Variable pay can work for individual, team, or organizational performance, perhaps as a bonus or some form of incentive payment. In executive compensation programs, stock options might be included. Variable pay generally requires a more fine-tuned performance appraisal system because it is outcome-oriented. For variable pay to generate worker interest and energy, the expectations must be realistic and the rewards for achieving these outcomes must be meaningful.

Nevertheless, from a financial standpoint, variable pay can be a very appealing alternative to base pay increase systems. Variable pay does not compound from year to year. Funds not spent can be reused in the current year or the next budget cycle. "Having employees re-earn their performance bonus each year creates a compelling reason for them to improve instead of relaxing into an entitlement mentality, which is often the result of base pay increase programs."[18]

Piece-rate pay is a form of variable pay in which worker output (number of widgets produced) is easily measurable and directly linked to his or her compensation. Pay can vary from day to day or hour to hour. Often, the worker receives a base rate. Added compensation is based on output above a predetermined standard. A piece-rate system can be administered without any formalized performance appraisal system.

Gainsharing aims to build productivity by sharing organizational gains from that productivity with those responsible, as in rewards for saving time or dollars. While gainsharing outcomes are often quantifiable, they can vary considerably from one work unit to another, making consistency in performance appraisal difficult.

An alternate structure, the fast-emerging use of **broadbands**, accommodates today's flatter organizational structure by eliminating narrowly defined jobs. Broadbanding emphasizes skills development and gives employees more freedom to move, either laterally or up and down, within a pay grade. An employee desiring to downshift to a less stressful position, for instance, could do so without suffering a drastic pay cut. Broadbanding recognizes that 21st-century employees often perform not one but several different jobs.[19]

Under broadbanding, pay decisions rest largely with managers— and the performance appraisal can be key. Entry-level employees with minimal qualifications begin at the first step of their range. But advancement depends on performance. All raises become individually determined merit raises. On the downside, managerial discretion opens possibilities of favoritism and abuse of the broadbanding structure.[20]

Incentives...or Disincentives?

More than 50 years ago, behavioral scientist Frederic Herzberg concluded that, "If you want people to do a good job, give them a good job to do."[21] Herzberg found that achievement and recognition are motivators. Pay becomes an issue only when it's inadequate, in which case it's a "dissatisfier." Today's employers seem boundless in their quest to give recognition. There are rewards for every reason. But however creative, how well do these perks work?

Alfie Kohn, a leading writer on money and motivation, asked whether the rewards work for the long-term interest of the company, or for some short-term personal goal? He indicated that non-cash rewards don't increase quality, productivity, or creativity. He pointed out that "one of the most thoroughly replicated findings in social psychology is that the more you reward people, the more they tend to lose interest in what they did to get the rewards. When interest declines, so does quality. 'You can get people to do more of something [or do it] faster for a little while if you provide an appealing reward. But no scientific study has ever found long-term enhancement of quality of work as a result of any reward system."[22]

"People seek, in a phrase, an enjoyable work environment," wrote Jeffrey Pfeffer.[23] Investigating successful companies characterized by motivated employees and low turnover despite competitive markets, he found that "one of the core values at each company is fun." In *Six Dangerous Myths About Pay*, he described what employees value at the SAS Institute in North Carolina:

Employees said they were motivated by SAS's unique perks— "plentiful opportunities to work with the latest and most up-to-date equipment and the ease with which they could move back and forth between being a manager and being an individual contributor. They also cited how much variety there was in the projects they worked on, how intelligent and nice the people they worked with were, and how much the organization cared for and appreciated them."[24]

Robert McNamara, former Secretary of Defense, once said, "Brains, like hearts, go where they are appreciated." The point that experts repeatedly underscore is that when core values are conveyed by recognition on many levels, when incentives capture organizational principles and genuinely honor employee dedication and talent, they can work exceptionally well. When awards are just exercises in giving awards, and an organization's core values are not defined and embedded at all levels of the organization, awards will tend to fall flat after initial interest. To sustain employee motivation, there needs to be more than a symbolic pat on the back…unless the pat is truly earned and the act of giving it is heartfelt.

Recognition matters. In *1001 Ways to Reward Employees*, Bob Nelson offers a treasure chest of positive and creative reinforcements—everything from low-cost, no-cost, and fun awards, to attendance and safety awards, team awards, self-development awards, and sales goal awards. Research by Dr. Gerald Graham throughout the United States revealed that the type of reward employees prefer is personalized, spur-of-the-moment recognition from their direct supervisors. And a survey of American workers found that, in fact, 63 percent ranked a pat on the back as a meaningful incentive.[25]

In addition to other opportunities, ensuring a series of informal evaluations throughout the year, rather than just the yearly appraisal "event," builds in the time to provide recognition that employees and supervisors value. One study found that just 41 percent of surveyed employees believe that the average company listens to employees' ideas. The average American worker makes only one or two suggestions per year, while the average Japanese worker submits hundreds.[26]

Three Scenarios

Applying compensation considerations to our three composite employees, Marilyn warrants extra incentives, Richard requires candor and support and, based on her continuing poor performance, Peg merits no increase.

Because Marilyn is such a consistently good performer, but already at the top of her range, she is slated for a substantial bonus. Her firm wants to keep her. As an added demonstration of appreciation, Marilyn might also receive a significant non-financial benefit. A thoughtful and very special perk might be free parking or attendance at her law firm's retreat.

Richard's history of solid performance serves him well during this difficult period when his ill parent needs his help. But work concerns need to be discussed openly. If Richard's work continues to slip, his next rate increase will be affected. For the time being, it's not. Richard also receives other support, including the opportunity to explore telecommuting, a compressed work week, or time off under the Family and Medical Leave Act.

Peg's poor performance still shows no improvement. Giving her any type of financial or non-financial recognition would send the wrong message. Acknowledging the problems, and documenting them as they occur, doesn't appear to be making a difference.

6

Rating Error Traps

I don't know that there are any shortcuts to doing a good job.
— Sandra Day O'Connor, first female justice
on the U.S. Supreme Court

When employees trust their supervisors to conduct fair and unbiased evaluations, their satisfaction with the system increases dramatically.[1] But the process must remain trustworthy; if it breaks down toward the end because of rating errors, the whole effort is tainted. Both employees and supervisors must be aware of what these errors are and how they affect performance evaluations. Employees need to stay vigilant, and managers' good intentions must be accompanied by the skill, understanding, and training required to reduce rating errors as much as possible.

Even then, it's difficult. Although software can support some types of evaluations, performance appraisals are a human process—conceived, developed, and administered by people. No evaluation comes with a flaw-free guarantee. Peter Drucker makes it clear that performance cannot be measured fully: "As each human being is unique, we cannot simply add them together, or subtract them from one another.... [T]o arrive at meaningful measurements is one of the greatest challenges to management."[2]

Goal-based systems are often seen as the best current option for rating performance, but they must be used carefully. The kinds of behaviors that are specified in the goal-setting process are exactly what the employee will tend to focus on in his or her work, so it's critical that these are the behaviors the organization wants to encourage.[3]

Examples can be drawn from the composite employees of the three scenarios used at the ends of chapters in this book. Because Marilyn takes great pride in being cited for outstanding interpersonal relationships, there is some danger that she may not insist that some work move as fast as required. Richard's goals of processing a high number of duplicating orders per week may undercut quality and, in fact, may hurt business. Although Peg's poor performance must be addressed at every level, it's possible that paying attention to effective telephone protocols is undercut by a responsibility such as supporting typing overloads. This is another instance in which customer service may suffer.

Rater Bias

Focus on the dynamics of worker characteristics appears to have surfaced close to a century ago. Workplace awareness of individual needs and differences goes back to at least the early 20th century. In England, the work of Charles Darwin popularized ideas that individuals differed from each other in ways that were important. In France, the work of Alfred Binet and Theophile Simon led to the development of the first intelligence tests, and during World War I several armies tried using these tests to better assign soldiers to jobs. By 1923, personnel management was spelling out how to match a person's skills and aptitudes with job requirements.[4]

Performance evaluations have been evolving since the early 20th century, when they were created, in part, to reduce the potential for labor unrest. Companies began introducing formal job analysis to aid in employee selection and rationalize the hodgepodge of wage rates that existed in many companies.[5]

Bias in the process is well documented. A 15-year study by Pennsylvania State University revealed a pattern of employment practices that historically helped men get promoted to upper-management positions. It showed that employers make decisions based on "impression management," the ability of employees to shape and manage a self-image that positively influences others. Women were shown to be "low self-monitors," that is, less concerned with crafting an impressionable image than men, whose "chameleon-like quality" helped them adapt to changing social climates. It was discovered that "when employee promotions are based on subjective evaluations rather than skills and talent, men have the edge, with a 15 percent higher chance of being promoted."[6]

Another study, at a Midwestern university, found that when viewing a female employee on video, students consistently gave her lower ratings on such characteristics as "dependability" and "ability to do the job" when she was pregnant than they did when she was shown five months later, even though her behavior was the same on both tapes.[7]

Evaluation problems also emerge because of perceptual differences in definitions. When words such as poor, fair, adequate, satisfactory, and excellent are used, the evaluation can be distorted. Exactly what does each mean? In comparison with whom? Is every employee being rated by the same standard?

Common Rating Errors

Halo effect. An error can occur when an outstanding quality that the employee posesses unjustifiably affects the entire rating. There is a difference between halo errors and a true halo, which is justified by across-the-board excellent performance. Some organizations ask raters to evaluate everyone on a single dimension before proceeding to the next. The aim is to encourage raters to focus on a particular dimension rather than overall performance. Another often-used method is "reverse wording," which structures forms so that a favorable answer for the first question might be 10 on a scale of one to 10, while a favorable response to the sixth question might be one on the same scale. Again, the evaluator is required to focus on each question separately. Favorable first impressions that stay intact despite evolving problems are sometimes attributed to the halo effect.

Horns effect. In this reversal of the halo effect, a negative dimension becomes the basis of the whole evaluation, and a poor rating emerges because the negative performance in one area casts a shadow on all the others. If a sales manager, for example, receives a poor rating because he or she turns in paperwork late, that rating might be extended to sales skills that are excellent. Careful documentation of sales closings through the year would be one way to correct that kind of unjustified evaluation.

Sunflower effect. Managers may worry that giving employees a rating of "average" will reflect poorly on themselves, and so give all their employees top ratings. But that can backfire: the managers' supervisors may question the ratings and conclude that the managers did not spend enough time on the review to do it carefully. During an exit interview at one association, the departing employee, when asked his perspective on performance appraisals, responded that they were a joke—despite his earning among the highest ratings in the entire association. "Don't get me wrong," he said. "I like the increases, but I'm not doing my best work. I want to learn more, and either my supervisor doesn't care about understanding the work of different employees, or she just doesn't care."

Leniency or harshness error. One rater may tend to be tougher or more lenient with employees than other managers, or several raters may all have different value systems. When appraisals apply words like "adequate" and "good," standards might not be defined clearly enough to ensure consistency throughout an organization. Some raters just tend to mark high; others low. It's often why employees report feeling as if they're back in school—and frustrated. Two employees performing similarly may receive quite different ratings from their respective supervisors simply because of these supervisors' tendencies to rate high or low. This error is also called positive or negative leniency. Evaluators report that positive leniency "motivates employees and makes them feel good."[8] They may justify negative leniency with the observation that "nobody's perfect." The tendency to make leniency errors is particularly strong when raters are rushed.[9] Raters may be asked to check their evaluations for a pattern toward leniency. One common remedy for this is to ask raters to distribute their ratings, with percentages designated for the number of employees rated as excellent, good, adequate, and poor. But this is a contrived solution and can unjustly place employees in false categories simply because their evaluators must respond to percentage demands.

Central tendency error. Some supervisors are reluctant to give high or low ratings. They rate all employees as average and fail to distinguish between the star performers and those who need specific support. Also termed "clustered ratings error" or "scale shrinking," this method absolves managers from having to make judgments. It's sometimes used by raters who feel they don't know an employee well enough to come up with an actual rating. Sticking to the middle makes these evaluations less useful for making personnel decisions such as promotions, salary increases, training, counseling, and even feedback. Raters who make a central tendency error can be shown the bigger picture so they understand how their ratings are distorting the evaluation process. Sometimes organizations ask that employees be ranked so they don't all end up in the middle. But imposing a bell curve disbursement of employees' ratings can create other problems. Forcing the hand of a manager in an effort to arrive at predetermined ratings, or at a distribution that supports the increased budget, is not fair to employees and can lead to serious morale and legal problems.

Sugar-coating error. Discussing concerns verbally isn't enough to evaluate performance well. Problems develop when supervisors talk at length about needs for improvement and other concerns, but just jot down a few general lines on the appraisal form itself. Everything communicated verbally should also appear in writing, and vice versa. If that is not done, and further action needs to be taken, the available documentation falls short. For example, an employee may consistently give other departments incorrect information, but her appraisal reads only, "more care is needed in communicating to others." That does not cover the full scope of concern.

Recency of events error. This error occurs when the rating is based on a recent events—good or bad— rather than the entire period that is to be reviewed. Alleviating this error is one excellent reason for ensuring ongoing documentation and discussion. Without these activities, raters can forget the last five months of behavior and evaluate just the past five weeks. Employees sometimes exploit this reality, becoming especially active and visible just before review time. But even if a supervisor documents performance effectively, employees will benefit from carrying a "picture" of their efforts during the review cycle into the appraisal meeting, particularly if he or she has shown improvement since the previous cycle.

Critical incidents effect. Similar to the halo and horns effects, this error distorts the overall review by giving undue emphasis to a single episode, positive or negative. No one incident should dominate the entire review cycle. An especially excellent or poor performance at any point in the cycle should not subsume performance during the rest of the cycle.

Contrast effect. When the evaluation of one employee affects that of another, it's known as a contrast error. Because every employee merits an appraisal based on individual performance, the contrast error skews the process. If a stellar performer, for example, is evaluated right before a good performer, the contrast might demote the second employee to just a fair rating. A contrast error can also result when the rater compares past and present performance. An employee rated "good" in one review might be rated "poor" in the next one, even though his or her performance would otherwise be rated fair.

Personal Bias Error. Bias has many faces—and none belongs in the appraisal. Some types of bias are readily apparent. But others are subtler, such as what's called a similarity error. This distortion occurs when a supervisor gives a higher rating to an employee simply because the two of them share similar characteristics, such as getting to work on time or being willing to work late. A supervisor may be totally unaware that he or she is even doing this. Longtime employees should be evaluated based on the quality of their performance, not on the number of years they have been with an organization. Ongoing, careful documentation, coupled with objective standards, goes a long way toward countering a bias error.

Stereotyping, or generalizing across a group, is tied to bias. Just like other forms of bias, stereotypical views can also be subtle. Not recognizing individual differences and assuming, for example, that all marketing directors are motivated and ambitious and that every engineer is highly analytical creates subjective standards that can lead to rating errors. There may also be perceptual difference errors shaped by the manager's experiences and perspectives. A teacher, for example, might be appraised based on the rater's classroom experiences rather than on his or her own teaching skills.

Low motivation error. Evidence shows that it is more difficult to obtain accurate appraisals when important rewards depend on the results.[10] When the stakes are high, supervisors may be reluctant to provide an unbiased appraisal for fear of hurting the employee's chances of receiving added compensation, a promotion, or other opportunity for professional growth.

Past anchoring errors. Employees get caught in this error when managers rate performances based on prior evaluations instead of taking a fresh look.

Sampling error. This error occurs when the evaluator rates an entire review cycle on the basis of just a small sample of an employee's work.

Varying standards error. When two or more employees perform similar work yet are held to different standards, the discrepancy distorts a fair and just evaluation process. One employee, for example, might be rated "good" for closing 65 percent of his or her sales while another employee documenting the same number of closings is rated only "fair."

Holding employees accountable when it's not their fault. Widespread negative evaluations probably mean that fault is with management, which is not holding all employees accountable. If, for example, documents from large numbers of staff tend to show up late at certain times, there may be problems with technology, not the employees. It's important to check that before appraisal time. Employees should also not be held accountable for work requirements they were never told about, a problem that can surface when work standards are set without referring to the job description and actual requirements. This error is tied closely to setting unrealistic objectives, such as holding employees accountable for work they're not trained for, or having them field multiple priorities with unrealistic deadlines, complete complex assignments without adequate research assistance, and similar misplaced goals.

Attribution bias. Distorted ratings occur when outstanding performance is attributed to factors external to the employee being rated, such as "great team support," but poor performance is perceived as the result of an employee's own behavior. Poor technological acumen, for example, might be attributed to lack of employee understanding, while excellent technological skills might be due to organizational training. In one instance, the employee is held accountable; in the second, an external factor gains the praise. A supervisor may want to grab credit for good performance. In other words, when work goes well, good management is credited. When it doesn't, poor employee performance is blamed.

Reducing Rating Errors

The following practices greatly reduce the errors in performance reviews:

Management Review

Performance appraisals should be reviewed by the manager's manager or the human resources department before the manager sits down with the employee. This helps ensure that the rating matches the narrative and that the overall assessment is justified. Being one step removed from the manager/employee relationship, the manager's manager can contribute the objective insight and constructive feedback needed to make necessary changes. The management review provides safeguards that are important to both the supervisor and the organization.

Training

"Research shows that training can minimize rating errors. When raters learned which data to focus on, how to interpret it, and how to use it to formulate judgments, ratings were more reliable and accurate than when there was no training or training incongruent with rating needs," wrote E.D. Pulakos.[11] The two most popular types of training programs are designed to help eliminate the kinds of errors described previously and to improve supervisors' observation and recording skills. While programs dealing with errors seem to eliminate many of them from ratings, there is much less evidence that this kind of training actually increases the accuracy of appraisals. Programs focused on observation and recording skills may offer greater improvements in accuracy than those that simply focus on errors, according to an article in *The Journal of Applied Psychology*.[12]

Regardless of the format, effective training conveys a full understanding of the evaluation process. It involves learning how to complete all materials, becoming a true player in appraisal sessions, being alert to legal implications, and leaving the door open to a continuing process. Trainers design sessions reflecting the particular culture and needs of organizations, with workshop activities that tackle the tough challenge of reducing rating errors.

Rater training serves to remind supervisors and employees of the importance of the appraisal process. It underscores that for every employee to receive the fairest rating possible, information must be reviewed responsibly, knowledgeably, and legally. Because it's not difficult for rating errors to creep into any performance evaluation, it's essential to be on guard against any distortion of the process.

Training will work only if supervisors are motivated and committed to applying it and organizational accountability is built into the process. Conducting high-quality, timely performance appraisals should, in fact, be a rated factor in the appraisals of supervisors.

Appeals Process

Most companies build employee response into the evaluation process. This may take the form of an employee-generated memo, but often it is an official response form that is attached to the written review. Sometimes happy employees will respond accordingly, but employees who are displeased with their ratings are more apt to express their reaction. Some organizations make sure those employees have another option: a complaint resolution process or formal grievance procedure.

Ensuring Checks and Balances

✓ Conduct rater training.
✓ Clarify the sequence of evaluation procedures.
✓ Ensure that the supervisor's supervisor signs off on all appraisals before they're given to employees.
✓ Build in time for the Human Resources department to conduct a second check.
✓ Provide a clear form inviting the employee to respond, in writing, to the review.
✓ Institute a formal appeals review, including a mediator if the employee desires one.

Smart companies believe that any employee with a complaint should have the opportunity to be heard and have the concern promptly and objectively reviewed and corrected, if necessary, with no fear of retaliation. Organizations support resolution through varying routes; some are two- or three-step processes, others are more extensive.

For any process to be effective, it should include an orderly and well-communicated system, specific steps and time frames that are followed by any employee with a similar issue. Conflict resolution processes begin with an employee putting his or her rebuttal in writing, then discussing those concerns with the immediate supervisor. The organization should designate in writing how many days the employee has to schedule and conduct this meeting and each subsequent meeting as necessary.

If the issue is not resolved by this point, a more formal process begins. An independent mediator might be brought into the process to facilitate a resolution as quickly as possible. If the employee remains dissatisfied, the supervisor can schedule a private meeting between the employee and the supervisor's supervisor. This meeting, too, should occur within a specified time, after which both managers write the results of their respective meetings on designated portions of the appraisal form. If an employee still seeks a resolution, he or she can meet with the next level of management. That individual looks into the matter and proposes a solution.

If the dispute is still unsettled, a panel of trained peers, guided by a mediator, can explore the information from both parties. The peers will make a decision within organizational parameters. Human resources and one of the top executives will review the panel's decision, either signing off on the decision and making it binding, or offering an alternative solution that all parties can live with.

Three Scenarios

The following evaluation incidents about Marilyn, Richard, and Peg demonstrate how easily rating errors can occur. Because Marilyn, a generally high performer, gets along well with everyone, her supervisor gives her an across-the-board "excellent" rating, without first reviewing her performance across the full range of rating categories (**halo effect**). As another example, one of Marilyn's key responsibilities during the appraisal cycle was to contract out construction work designed to expand the office in time for new attorneys to come on board. Despite contractor delays, Marilyn made sure the job was finished on deadline. As significant as it was, her supervisor allowed this one achievement to color all others (**critical incidents effect**).

Richard's parent was rushed to the hospital two weeks before his performance review. Unexpectedly away from the office, he never delegated his work, and part of an important assignment slipped through the cracks. This incident stayed fresh in the mind of his supervisor, who gave him an overall low performance rating despite Richard's other positive achievements during the appraisal cycle (**recency of events error**). In another instance, Richard's duplicating department budget was sliced, despite a commitment to a client to produce work requiring technology that now had to be placed on hold. Told to deliver the work anyway, Richard had to outsource the work, then was held responsible for the budget deficit (**unrealistic objectives error**).

Despite Peg's continuing poor performance, her supervisor keeps trying to support her, postponing or completely derailing the need to fire her. She's also concerned that a poor rating will affect her supervisor's review of her as a manager, so she gives Peg a higher rating than her performance deserves, a disservice to Peg, her supervisor, and the advertising agency that employs them (**sunflower effect**).

Performance-Review Training Exercises for Large and Small Groups

Open by asking participants to generate a list of why performance appraisals are important; this jump-starts thinking about the review's long-term importance *before* focusing on the form.

Ask what documentation is needed to arrive at a fair rating, including last year's goals, significant accomplishments, job description, work examples, observation notes, input from others, employee's self-assessment, and any other job- or goal-related information based on performance that should not be overlooked. Build a discussion about the value and pitfalls of each item.

Stage a role-play in which an "employee" works through each section of the evaluation form, with ratings based on examples drawn from the documentation. The "employee" challenges the ratings, providing the "supervisor" a chance to clarify why and how he or she arrived at the ratings. Sprinkled through the explanation are blatant, then subtler, examples of rating errors. Participants have sheets listing many rating errors. Individually, then as a group, they are identified.

Small-group exercises are useful, too. After a general explanation of rating errors, written scenarios are distributed and participants break into small groups to identify the source of problems. The larger group can then convene to discuss reactions to the process of identifying, then correcting, errors. The group can discuss the best ways for supervisors and employees to spot rating errors before they take hold.

7

When Appraisals Derail

Tell me, I will forget,
Show me, I may remember,
Involve me, I will understand

—Chinese Proverb

What can send an appraisal discussion off track? There are many possible culprits. One of the most serious is an absence of mini-conversations on performance throughout the cycle. The result is often surprise and disappointment for the employee once they finally hear the manager's assessment during the anual discussion.

But there can be a number of other reasons for negative discussions. This is the time to conduct what author Jim Collins calls an "autopsy without blame," an open, honest look at the reasons for derailment and their root causes "in a climate where the truth can be heard."[1]

Such an environment requires not just hearing but "active listening." On the supervisor's part, it requires a clear explanation of purpose, a willingness to establish trust, the openness to invite the

Blueprint for Positive Appraisals

✓ Give feedback that is specific and behavioral.

✓ Describe the behavior's impact on the team or the attainment of the person's goals.

✓ Express your observations calmly.

✓ Avoid overwhelming the other person with too much feedback all at once.

✓ Let the person present his or her side of the problem, engage in a dialogue, and avoid any tendency to lecture.

✓ Focus on the future.

✓ Clearly identify the pay-off.

✓ Provide the appropriate balance of positive and negative feedback. Offer to help improve.

✓ Express empathy when you perceive discouragement. Acknowledge that change does not happen overnight and can be difficult.

employee into the feedback process, and a genuine effort to understand what the employee is saying. Feedback must be treated as information, not as a value judgment.[2]

On the employee's part, it takes much of the same, with demonstrated willingness to become actively engaged in owning the appraisal.

In *Coaching*, Ferdinand F. Fournies emphasized that "[i]t's important to remember that this is a discussion: two people are participating in a conversation." Supervisors shouldn't lecture or answer their own questions. "[E]mployees have learned that if the boss asks them a question and they don't answer it, the boss answers his or her own question." If, after a reasonable period, the employee still hasn't answered, the supervisor can ask if the employee wants the question repeated.[3]

In working toward next steps, Fournies cautions that "[i]f you argue the merits of ideas as they are given, you are wasting *idea-giving time*. If you reject ideas as they are given, you could be punishing *idea-giving behavior*....Generating ideas depends on the interaction of ideas," and the process needs patience to most effectively run its course. The best ideas may even rebound from the bad or seemingly trivial ones. [4]

According to *The Successful Manager's Handbook*, "Successful negotiation engages people, especially those who have ongoing interaction, in seeking and identifying a solution satisfactory to all. When both sides are open to winning on some points and compromising or losing on others, they are more likely to arrive at a solution they can accept and support. When a clear winner and a clear loser emerge from a negotiation session, hard feelings are likely to result. The "loser" may undermine the solution, and it is possible that no one will "win" in the long run.[5]

For example, negotiating ideas can work like this:

Supervisor: *It's time to start the inventory count next week.*

Employee: *I created a new system for us to us.*

Supervisor: *I'm not convinced...I've been using our old system for years.*

Employee: *It has some great features I think you'll like, and it lets us get the job done quicker.*

Supervisor: *Let's do this: continue to use the old tracking forms, but add the new columns for the extra data you're gathering. We can review it together and decide how to proceed. Sound fair?*

Because any misunderstanding can be a springboard for an inaccurate perception, it's critical to correct it before the inaccurate perception takes hold and spawns more.

Natalie Loeb, a New Jersey executive coach, calls feedback a gift. "It's hard," she says, "to correct something when you're not clear what it is."

Employee: *I know why you called me in.*

Supervisor: *Why do you think?*

Employee: *I came in late again yesterday. It's that bus. It always runs late.*

Supervisor: *Yes, Jessica, I am concerned about that. But the real problem is that we have a team here. You're on the team. If you can come in late, it's not fair to the others. The same thing applies* *to the weekly report. I depend on everyone's feedback to move it to the board. So do you see what the problem really is here?*

Employee: *I'm not sure.*

Supervisor: *I want to hear what you think.*

Employee: *I guess I need to be more on time with things.*

Supervisor: *Why, do you think?*

Employee: *I'm part of the whole team here. And I'm creating holes.*

Supervisor: *You say it well, Jessica. Can I count on you now to fill them?*

Employee: *I'm on board.*

In *That's Not What I Meant*, Deborah Tannen—a widely published linguistics professor at Georgetown University in Washington, D.C.—called attention to "some typical ways the conversational signals of pacing, pausing, loudness, and pitch are used to carry on the business of taking turns in conversation; relating ideas to each other and showing what the point is; and showing how we feel about what we're saying and about the person we're saying it to. These are the signals that combine with what is said to make up the devices we use to show we're listening, interested, sympathetic, or teasing. Normally invisible, these conversational signals and devices are the silent and hidden gears that drive conversation."[6]

"We don't pay attention to these gears unless something seems to have gone wrong," Tannen wrote. "Then we may ask, 'What do you *mean* by that?' And even then we don't think in terms of the signals 'Why did your pitch go up?'—but in terms of intentions— 'Why are you angry?' "

Derailed appraisals can indicate a struggle to say what we mean. But "say what you mean, and mean what you say" is only half of it. How the information is taken in, and what occurs in the translation, is where trip-ups also occur. This is especially true if blocks to listening are in play.

The Hostile Employee

Toni, the front office desk clerk, doesn't accept responsibility for substandard performance and gets very angry and defensive during the appraisal discussion. She disagrees with her review and blames other employees while speaking with her supervisor, Lydia.

Tips for the Supervisor

✓ Let Toni respond.

✓ Listen.

✓ Ask Toni questions to find out the real reason for her anger.

> *Lydia: It's time to discuss a few areas where you can concentrate some additional effort.*
>
> *Toni: What are you talking about?*
>
> *Lydia: Well, I have a few samples of the monthly reports here. There are some gaps where room charges needed to be added before you submitted them.*
>
> *Toni: Just a minute. That wasn't my fault!*
>
> *Lydia: Tell me how you think the process failed. Is there something else bothering you?*

✓ Restate your point of view.

✓ Let Toni know that it is difficult to continue the conversation with so much emotion.

> *Lydia: Toni, I'd like to do some problem-solving with you here.*
>
> *Toni: I think you're just trying to blame me. You know very well that the kitchen is responsible for getting that information to me. Why should I have to remind them when it's due? They're adults! You just want to criticize me.*
>
> *Lydia: I don't want to criticize you. I want you to be the best employee around here.*
>
> *Toni: Right.*

✓ Decide whether it is prudent to continue the performance appraisal meeting.

✓ If not, reschedule. If possible, establish some ground rules for the rest of the meeting and continue.

> *Lydia: Toni, I can see that you're upset. These discussions about performance are not meant to do that. Why don't we meet again later this afternoon, at 3 p.m., and we'll start over? I'll expect you to approach the topic of work problems constructively. And we'll both come to that meeting with some solutions. Is that a deal?*

✓ Be ready to share with Toni examples that support the ratings and/or narrative comments on the evaluation form.

✓ Let Toni know that you will give her resources to help her in her work and be available to provide guidance.

✓ Make sure she understands that she will be responsible for her performance. If she is able to turn things around, you will be her biggest supporter.

The Too-Quiet Employee

Joe, the mail clerk, accepts his review without saying a word and prepares to leave before there has been much discussion. His supervisor, Charlie, thinks the review is fair and balanced, acceptable overall. It seems that Joe is agreeing with him either to end the session quickly or to please his boss.

Tips for the Supervisor

✓ Probe to see what Joe's feelings are.

✓ Make sure he understands the performance issues.

✓ Ask open-ended questions to encourage him to talk.

> *Charlie: I've covered all the points I wanted to go over with you, Joe, but you haven't said much. I was hoping for more of a two-way conversation about your performance.*

> *Joe: Well...*
>
> *Charlie: Why don't you give me your reaction to what I've said?*
>
> *Joe: It was all fine, Charlie, really. I agree.*
>
> *Charlie: Okay. Let's talk about some future projects for you. What would interest you?*
>
> *Joe: Whatever you want me to focus on is fine with me. You're the boss, Charlie.*

- ✓ Tell Joe that he will be expected to talk 60 percent of the meeting time.
- ✓ Listen.
- ✓ Allow silences.
- ✓ Reschedule if necessary.

> *Charlie: No, Joe, that's not how this works. This is your performance appraisal, a discussion pulling together all the talks we've had over the last six months. It's time for reflection, for planning, and for some good feedback, both ways. Maybe I wasn't clear about what I hoped this meeting could achieve. Why don't we reschedule for tomorrow morning and we'll pick up there? I'll expect you to do most of the talking, Joe, so be ready. Give some thought as to what you'd like to do next quarter during the remodeling of the mailroom. Remember, Joe, I'm going to do a lot of listening not talking. See you then.*

- ✓ Have more frequent meetings with Joe.

The New Supervisor

Tara was recently brought in from the outside to be the senior vice president of human resources. Lucas, director of employee relations, wanted that position and felt he was qualified. He was very disappointed that he wasn't selected and has not accepted Tara in her role as her supervisor.

Tips for the Supervisor

✓ Anticipate resistance.

✓ Respect feelings.

✓ Be patient.

✓ Avoid confrontation or downplay conflict; try to refuse resistance.

✓ Give adjustment time.

✓ Show yourself as a supportive boss; remain positive.

> **Tara:** *It's time to have your performance appraisal, Lucas.*
>
> **Lucas:** *You haven't been here long enough to assess my work.*
>
> **Tara:** *That's true. So I won't be doing a full appraisal at this time. But I wanted to share the form your previous supervisor left. As we work together in the months ahead, I'll be able to see the good work you do first-hand. I'm looking forward to it.*

✓ Stress common ground/areas of agreement; build rapport.

✓ Be clear about expectations.

✓ Stress mutual benefits for department.

> **Tara:** *I know we both want to be involved in the most effective and efficient HR operation. And I think we could make a formidable team. I'd like us to set some reachable goals for you and your group for the next quarter. Let's examine the turnover statistics and supervisory training sessions for the last year. I'd like your thoughts on how we can reduce the number of unemployment claims and terminations.*
>
> **Lucas:** *I have a lot of ideas.*
>
> **Tara:** *Great. I was hoping you would. Let's get started. This will be the first in a series of meetings for us.*

✓ Keep communication open. Cultivate the relationship.

The Settled-In Employee

Harvey, the marketing copywriter, is a long-term employee who has not received honest feedback regarding his less-than-stellar performance for years. Dorinne, his new supervisor, has taken her responsibility of preparing an honest appraisal very conscientiously and has to review some areas of unsatisfactory and marginal performance. She has tried to provide open and honest feedback throughout the performance period but Harvey has refused to hear it.

Tips for the Supervisor

- ✓ Show appreciation for the value Harvey adds.
- ✓ Ask Harvey how he thinks things are going. His responses may help you decide how to proceed.
- ✓ Give specific examples of his performance that fell short of expectations.
- ✓ Review a few earlier conversations regarding his performance.

> **Dorinne:** *Harvey, you've been with the department quite a while, and you've seen a lot of changes. I rely on you to give me some of that archival knowledge you have on so many projects. I value that. As we discussed through the year, there are a few areas of your performance that need some attention.*

> **Harvey:** *With all due respect, Dorinne, you're my fifth supervisor in seven years, and everyone else thought I was doing just fine.*

> **Dorinne:** *I can't comment on how others might have evaluated your work, Harvey. But I need you to know that I take this responsibility quite seriously. I want to continue to give you honest feedback to help you be even more of an asset to our unit. I think there are some things we can work on together. I'd like that. For example, I have some ideas that might help you get your response rate up. Your last three packages didn't meet the target.*

- ✓ Restate expectations.
- ✓ Ask open-ended questions to determine how Harvey feels about his job.
- ✓ Reinforce his strengths.
- ✓ Develop a plan for improvement together.
- ✓ Express support that Harvey can meet the expectations.
- ✓ Establish a follow-up process.

> **Dorinne:** *I've gotten the conference schedule for the copywriters' seminar next month. Perhaps a few of the technical sessions would be helpful. You need to get your response rate up to 10 percent. Which sessions might be most helpful, do you think? I think you'll be able to bump up those numbers. Let's review the next package together, okay?*

The Surprise Appraisal

Paul is a "hands-off" director rarely available to his manager, Bernie. It's now time for the performance review meeting, and Bernie has no idea what Paul will say. There has been no ongoing dialogue throughout the performance period, and Bernie is looking forward to some constructive feedback.

Tips for the Employee

- ✓ Don't expect too much.
- ✓ Actively solicit feedback.
- ✓ Hit the high points of your performance; be brief and focused; don't be long-winded; don't overwhelm.
- ✓ Present a well-documented self-appraisal.
- ✓ Get clarification on expectations.

> **Paul:** *You're doing fine, Bernie, just fine.*
>
> **Bernie:** *Thanks, Paul. I've been looking forward to hearing more about how I'm doing.*

Paul: *More?*

Bernie: *Well, details about what I did that really worked; what I could have improved on. And of course, future projects....*

Paul: *I see.*

Bernie: *I've prepared a self-appraisal for you to check. I've highlighted my major responsibilities at the top, along with some of the major projects for the last six months. Could we go through it briefly?*

✓ Read clues as to when Paul is ready for the meeting to end.

Bernie: *Two last questions, because I know you need to get to another meeting: Do you have specific deliverables for me next quarter? And what specifically would you advise me to do to get ready for my next step professionally? I value your opinion. I'd be available to pick up this discussion later if that works better for you. These meetings help me so much.*

✓ Accept that details aren't important to Paul.

✓ Try for brief follow-up meetings in the future; express how they help you.

8

Keep It Legal!

By Diane Gold

Fiction is obliged to stick to possibilities. Truth isn't.
—Mark Twain, American humorist and author

In a legal battle, even emerging as a winner may feel like a half-hearted victory after so much time, money, and emotion have been invested in the effort. An employer can use performance appraisals to defend against a claim, can be the focus of an employee complaint, or can be used as evidence in legal disputes tied to other employment decisions. If an employee is part of a "protected" class, such as being age 40 or older, and an appraisal statement reads, "Carl needs to show more energy," that might be construed as an age-related criticism.

When another employment decision is the issue, such as an employer's alleged failure to promote an employee, that employee might point to outstanding appraisals to show reason for promotion. If an employee alleges that his or her job was terminated for a discriminatory reason, then, too, the employee may point to positive appraisals to show that the termination is not justified.

Avoid Challenges

To avoid lawsuits alleging discriminatory appraisals, it's vital that the performance objectives and the rating itself are consistent. If, for example, an employee is rated on elements that were not clearly articulated, he or she is more likely to allege that the rating is unfair. If there is no clear basis for the rating, the employee may assume that the reason for the low or negative rating is based on race, religion, sex, national origin, or another illegal categorization.

As long as rating elements are objective, a manager will have an easier time defending a challenged rating. If an employee is rated on "friendliness," for instance, what does that really mean? What is friendly to one person might be annoying to another. Subjective criteria such as attitude, personality, or demeanor are inherently difficult to measure. Examples of more objective evaluation factors include measuring how many sales an employee made, how often a copywriter has met deadlines, or whether a vice president has brought projects in on budget 90 percent of the time. While it's not always possible to quantify rating elements with numbers, aiming for objectivity makes it easier for the manager to prepare the rating and easier for the employee to understand it. Quantifying those elements may also keep the rating from being challenged.

It's also vital that supervisors keep a running file of notes on their employees' performances. This ensures a contemporaneous performance record with specific examples to cite. With carefully kept records in hand, supervisors won't have to dig into their memories and are more likely to produce an appraisal that fairly reflects the whole appraisal period, not just recent events.

EEO Compliance

Staying out of legal trouble means rating employees equitably, based on their skills and abilities. Federal law prohibits considering an employee's race, color, age, sex, religion, national origin, pregnancy, or disability in all employment decisions, including performance evaluations. State, county, or city laws, and local rules or ordinances, must also be followed.

The most legally damaging comments in an appraisal are those that blatantly indicate that the rater factored in a protected category. The focus must be on performance only. Also, managers must be trained in understanding and complying with employment laws.

Another problem is giving employees higher ratings than they would otherwise receive—simply because a supervisor likes them, has a personal friendship with them, or is attracted to them. Ratings that factor in personality conflicts can also trigger legal trouble. How much an employee is liked or disliked does not belong in the appraisal process, and supervisors must keep personal feelings in check to prevent claims of bias down the road.

Don't Provide Evidence

Plaintiffs in employment cases often try to show that they do not deserve undesirable treatment by using positive performance appraisals. An employee questioning a demotion or low compensation will undoubtedly use positive performance ratings to prove that the negative action is unfair and unwarranted. If managers inflate ratings, they can find that their hands are tied later, when they need to let someone go.

In a case of alleged discriminatory termination, employees with a history of positive reviews can be expected to use those reviews or ratings as evidence on their behalf. In one age discrimination case, a court reasoned that the employer's defense—that the plaintiff was a poor performer—was not substantiated by written ratings. The court ultimately concluded that using poor job performance as a reason for his RIF (reduction in force) was "an afterthought."[1]

What the Courts Say

In analyzing discrimination cases, including ones involving performance appraisals, courts follow legal analyses and case law developed pursuant to Title VII of the Civil Rights Act of 1964. Three areas of evidence are analyzed in discrimination cases. First, the employee is required to prove a *prima facie* case that is considered to raise an inference of discrimination. Second, the employer must come forward with why it took the action in question. Third, in order to prevail on his or her claim, the employee must establish that the employer's reason is not valid, or is merely a pretext for a discriminatory motive.

Establishing a *prima facie* case of prohibited discrimination means employees must prove three factors:

1. They are part of a protected class.
2. They have suffered an adverse employment action.
3. They have been treated less favorably than someone who is similarly situated who does not belong to their protected class.

When Is a Bad Appraisal an "Adverse Action"?

As the second factor of a *prima facie* case, employees must prove that their rating constitutes an "adverse action." Poor performance appraisals, along with other business decisions that might make an employee unhappy, aren't necessarily considered adverse actions under the law. Courts generally look at whether the action at issue is a "tangible employment action" that amounts to "a significant change in employment status, such as hiring, firing, failing to promote, reassignment with significantly different responsibilities, or a decision causing a significant change in benefits."[2] While a lower than expected rating itself may not rise to this level, the negative monetary effect of such a rating, such as a lower bonus, cash award, or salary, can often be considered an adverse action for making out a valid claim of discrimination. For instance, in a Washington, D.C. case in which the plaintiff received a bonus of $807 based on a rating of "excellent," instead of the $1,355 bonus that her coworker received with a rating of "outstanding," the court determined that this difference constituted an adverse action for the purposes of presenting a *prima facie* case of discrimination under Title VII.[3]

To complete their *prima facie* case, employees must show that they were treated less favorably than someone in a similar position who is not part of his or her protected group. If employees can prove all the elements of the *prima facie* case, the burden then shifts to employers to defend their decision.

Courts will frown upon documentation of poor performance made after the appraisal is conducted. Created "after the fact," such documentation might be viewed by courts as an attempt to cover up a rating that was not based on appropriate or lawful criteria.

When Is an Inconsistent Rating Discriminatory "Pretext"?

After a *prima facie* case is established, the court raises a presumption that the motivation behind the employment action was "prohibited discrimination" against the employee because she or he belongs to a protected group.[4] At this point, the employer can overcome that presumption by articulating a valid reason for taking the action.[5] If the employer does so, the employee can introduce evidence tending to prove that the employer's reason is not valid and is instead really pretext, with the real motive having been the prohibited discrimination that the employee originally alleged.

"Pretext," in the context of job performance ratings, means that the employer is not being truthful and that the actual reason for the negative employment action is either discriminatory or otherwise unlawful or inappropriate. Pretext can be shown in several ways: inconsistency in the evidence the employer presents or between the rating and the actual performance, or a difference in treatment between employees relating to the appraisal process. For instance, if only some employees receive ratings, if employees with similar jobs are rated on different criteria, or if some employees receive extensive explanations of their ratings while others get minimal feedback, the employee can strengthen his or her legal case by pointing to the difference in treatment.

When ratings are inconsistent, there is inequity—and legal vulnerability. If a lawsuit is brought, a court may find that "[d]eviation from established policy or practice may be evidence of pretext."[6] Once a court finds that the employer's defense is pretextual, it can infer that the employer is trying to cover up a discriminatory motive. Alternatively, courts have ruled that if an employee who suddenly gets a bad rating has a new supervisor, the sole fact that the new supervisor's expectations differ from those of previous supervisors will not necessarily prove pretext.[7] Courts will also look at substantial changes in an employee's work responsibilities as an explanation for deviation from a pattern of generally positive appraisals.

For an employee to ultimately prevail, he or she must prove his or her case by a "preponderance of the evidence"—that is, "that degree of relevant evidence which a reasonable mind, considering the record as a whole, might accept as sufficient to support a conclusion that the matter asserted is more likely to be true than not true."[8]

Special Considerations

Disability

Sometimes an employer gets into legal trouble when a supervisor thinks that a bad rating might be the result of a mental or physical problem and asks the employee health-related questions. A court could interpret these types of questions as evidence of disability discrimination. However, if the employee reveals and/or explains that he or she has a medical issue that requires attention, the supervisor should handle the matter with sensitivity and refer the employee to personnel who are trained to handle these types of issues (for example, an employee assistance program, a staff nurse, or the human resources department). The message here is that the supervisor should focus on the performance deficiency itself, without speculating about the reason for its occurrence.

Retaliation

Retaliation claims arise when employees allege they received a lower rating than they otherwise would have, because they filed an EEO complaint or engaged in other activity that is considered "protected."[9] Employers need to be particularly careful about fairness in rating an employee who has engaged in such activity. It is generally easier for an employee to prevail on a retaliation claim than to prove the initial claim of discrimination itself.

In order to prove a retaliation claim, employees generally must prove:

1. They engaged in a protected activity.
2. Their employer was aware of the protected activity.
3. The employer took adverse action against them.
4. There was a causal connection between the protected activity and the adverse action.[10] Demonstrating that the adverse action followed the protected activity within a short period of time is one way to establish a causal connection.

Employees and their attorneys might scrutinize a rating that is received after an EEO complaint was filed. If the rating is lower than the employee received in previous years, or the language reflects hostility or a previously absent critical tone, there is often fertile ground for a new EEO complaint based on the rating.

After an employee files a discrimination charge, or is otherwise involved in a discrimination case, supervisors must take special care to treat him or her fairly. Although it might be difficult to focus on fairness if the employer considers the employee's claim unjust, supervisors must work to keep any acrimonious feelings in check.

Team Evaluations

All individuals participating in evaluations must understand and be trained in the process, as well as in EEO laws, documentation, and consistency. This is especially important because if an employee ever challenges an evaluation and/or the appraisal process, a court could see a derogatory or otherwise inappropriate comment by one of several evaluators as tainting the entire process. Also, an employer's efforts to train supervisors on how to comply with employment laws is an important part of defending against an EEO claim.

E-Mails and Other Documentation

When an employee challenges a performance appraisal in court, his or her attorney will be able to access and review a wealth of information, any or all of which could shape the court's decision.

Documentation includes previous performance appraisals, other employees' appraisals, and memos and e-mails concerning performance. E-mails are often the evidence of choice in employment discrimination cases because people generally take less care when writing them than when writing official correspondence or documents on company letterhead. Take heed, or your hard drive may show up in court. Here again, training is vital.

Test Your Legal IQ

- ✓ Are the rating factors objective?
- ✓ Do employees understand what is expected of them?
- ✓ Are you documenting performance during the entire rating period?
- ✓ Are you communicating with the employee about his or her performance during the course of the rating period?
- ✓ Are you spending the same amount of time and attention on each employee's performance?
- ✓ Have supervisors received training on implementing the performance process?
- ✓ Have supervisors received basic EEO training?
- ✓ Is the appraisal free from extraneous comments and personal opinions?
- ✓ Have you given specific examples on the appraisal to demonstrate the employee's strengths and/or weaknesses?
- ✓ Are you rating performance solely on the bases of skills and abilities?
- ✓ Are you favoring or disfavoring any employee for reasons unrelated to his or her performance?
- ✓ Are ratings consistent in process and procedure throughout the organization?
- ✓ Are ratings reviewed (and signed) by a more senior manager?
- ✓ Are ratings discussed with the employee so that he or she understands any deficiencies?

9

Performance Reviews in a Changing World

We shape our tools, and thereafter, our tools shape us.
—Marshall McLuhan, visionary educator and the "father of the electronic age," who declared, "The medium is the message."

We're experiencing what *Future Shock* author Alvin Toffler might call "an exclamation point in history,"[1] an era in which old barriers fall and there is vast reorganization of the production and distribution of knowledge and the symbols used to communicate it.[2]

Fast changes in today's work climate—flextime, telecommuting, job-sharing, improved training, and grouping employees by team, among many others—make it feasible to examine a fresh, fluid approach. A lagging economy and deep staff cuts make it a necessity.

Still not easy or even understandable in many traditional work settings, performance appraisals, too, need to adapt to change, especially with a workforce that is becoming both older and younger. A decade ago, in private industry, employees aged 55 or older constituted 11.9 percent of the working population. In 2000, that figure jumped to 12.9 percent. By 2010, it's projected to leap to an estimated

Psychological Turnover

"Retention issues are changing with the market," Dr. Beverly Kaye (co-author of *Love 'Em or Lose 'Em: Getting Good People to Stay*) told a Society for Human Resource management forum. Rather than physically walking out the door, she said, staff may "check out" by abandoning motivation and productivity, which creates "psychological turnover."[7] Although talented staff may stay with an organization during a sluggish job market, to hold them over the long run and boost their performance, Kaye recommended:

✓ Know that employers spend three times as much to recruit as they do to retrain.

✓ Understand that people stay in jobs for reasons beyond pay—employers must pay competitive salaries and offer an appealing workplace culture.

✓ Understand why staff stay or leave—conduct periodic "stay interviews," not just exit interviews.

✓ Make retention everyone's job.

✓ Recognize that mentoring is central to retention.

✓ Recognize that there will always be a higher bidder.

16.9 percent.[3] And just as baby boomers made their mark on the business world, 44 million Gen Xers are doing the same. Moving up fast are the Gen Ys. Born between 1979 and 1994, they're now "entering the workforce in earnest, with a lot of raw energy, unbridled enthusiasm, and the skills and experience of much older workers."[4] Gen Ys "live to be trained" and "absolutely thrive on recognition."[5]

With matrix management, work groups, team projects, multiple raters, multiple supervisors, and more workplace innovations, the team mindset is accelerating. Like so many of today's personnel practices, work by team isn't new. Sanford Jacoby, a professor of management at UCLA, reported that "self-managing work teams were evident in the 1870s, when groups of workers negotiated with owners for tonnage rates for each job, then decided on pay distribution, whom to hire, and how to organize and train for the job."[6] What is new is the prevalence of the team focus. Teamwork is not just a buzz word, but a concept that is spreading through organizational structures. In some cases, as in matrix management, it is changing those structures, injecting a new zest into organizations. Business as usual is getting a facelift.

Collaboration: Not an Ideal, But an Expectation

Even given the tools to retain good staff, an organization must have the will to apply them. Smart companies manage change by embracing it. As one CEO put it, "No matter what I've faced, personally or professionally, what keeps me going is a passage from *The Life and Letters of Charles Darwin*: 'It's not the strongest or the smartest that survive, but the ones most adaptable to change.'"[8] Duke Ellington put it another way: "Life has two rules: Number one, never quit. Number two, always remember number one."[9]

A company that prizes close teamwork and continuing feedback, despite its rapid growth developed an employee evaluation program characterized by quarterly reviews. "The whole idea of having an evaluation is to help you improve your performance," said Anil Chouhan, a supervisor there. "But if you're going to change behavior, you have to get the information to do it in a timely fashion—this way, you can decide that you need to work on these particular things over the next three months, and quickly see the results."

Another large company is working to shift appraisals away from merely measuring results. Using the process to build teamwork among employees and supervisors, it views management as "a function, not a class," which mitigates performance appraisal anxiety.

Yet another manufacturing firm combines objective and subjective performance measures into a single, integrated system. Its middle managers follow a "management by objectives" process in which performance is tied to indicators such as profit and debt objectives, customer service, and increasing sales in a particular market. Meeting objectives earns them sizable bonuses if their division also meets its objectives. Half of one division's managers might meet all their performance goals, but if the other half doesn't, none of them receive a bonus. That's a strong and measurable incentive for them to work together as a team.

Managing Change

In order to manage change, *The Successful Manger's Handbook* advises that you:

- ✓ Know the organization's current situation within its field.
- ✓ Develop a clear picture, or vision, of where it needs to go.
- ✓ Set specific goals and dates by which to achieve that vision.
- ✓ Outline the transition process in detail: Determine what needs to be done to achieve the desired change. The organization's subsystems of people, structure, technology, and tasks need to be directed to be compatible with the change.
- ✓ Develop and execute the plan for managing the transition.[10]

Jump-Starting Results

In the *Harvard Business Review on Change*, Robert H. Schaffer and Harvey A. Thomson state, "there is no reason for senior-level managers to acquiesce when their people plead they are already accomplishing just about all that can be accomplished, or that factors beyond their control are blocking accelerated performance improvement...Instead management needs to recognize there is an abundance of both unexploited capability and dissipated resources in the organization."[11]

Here's how they suggest driving new opportunities and jump-starting good results:

- ✓ Ask each unit to set and achieve a few ambitious, short-term performance goals. Every organization can improve with resources at hand. There might be faster turnaround time on customer requests, test of a managerial process, or cost savings.
- ✓ Periodically review progress, capture the essential learning, and reformulate strategy. Learn what is and isn't actually working. Fresh insights can generate new support, changed methods, and the confidence that comes from overhauling obsolete practices.
- ✓ Institute the changes that work—and discard the rest. Integrate the practices and technologies that contribute most to performance improvement.
- ✓ Create the context and identify the crucial business challenges. Establish a broader, strategic framework to guide continuing improvement.

Making Convictions Operational

Adapting performance reviews, even developing and implementing them effectively to begin with, never occurs in a vacuum. The broader work climate must embrace those needs. And the will to do that begins at the top—possibly after some convincing stops on the way up. But once a CEO understands the value of holding managers accountable for having ongoing workplace conversations, it's up to managers to turn that business philosphy into a robust performance-management system. Doing so requires communication, more communication, training and monitoring, and assessment. It takes, as Toffler put it, "thinking about 'big things' while you're doing 'small things,' so that all the small things go in the right direction."[12]

Championing the big things, such as organizational vision, takes many routes, all of which can help shape a positive performance appraisal process.

Communication

Leaders talk about leadership, usually enthusiastically. Microsoft Chairman Bill Gates said, "What I do best is spread my enthusiasm."[13] Microsoft CEO Steve Ballmer said, "The end point must be exciting enough to stir thousands to uncommon effort."[14] Former Chairman and CEO Herb Kelleher explained that Southwest Airlines gives employees the "opportunity to be a maverick. You don't have to fit into a constraining mold—you can have a good time."[15] Asked by a *BusinessWeek* columnist to sum up why he had been so successful at GE, former CEO Jack Walsh said, "My main job was developing talent. I was a gardener providing water and nourishment."[16]

Still, a survey conducted jointly by the Society for Human Resource Management and Personnel Decisions International found that 22 percent of participants said the greatest challenge they face is a lack of support from top management. Forty-two percent of the organizations that took part reported that executives do not even bother to review the performance management systems currently in place.[17]

As underscored throughout this book, almost everything an organization does tells its employees how much they count. For employees to feel valued, they must be valued. Expecting them to be on board with the organizational mission means they must genuinely be a part of that mission, and understand how. Vision needs to dovetail with recognition. A performance appraisal that recaps a continuing dialogue says the employee is vital to moving forward toward the vision. A perfunctory annual review says the opposite.

Organizations invite two-way communications in innumerable ways—from daily e-mails, chat rooms, and town hall meetings, to Friday pizza parties, more formal meetings, and sit-downs with the CEO. Some companies conduct anonymous surveys, asking such questions as "What's the best thing about working here?" "What three things would you change?" and "What makes you proud to be here?" At a company in Sydney, Australia, an employee was chosen by lottery and asked, "What would you do if you were CEO for a day?"

Welcoming employees to articulate values can be especially helpful in advance of a corporate restructuring, planning a product launch, designing new symbols, or perhaps redesigning of the appraisal process. Management consultants and authors James C. Collins and Jerry I. Porras often recommend "a Mars Group," a diverse group of employees they call "a representative slice of the company's genetic code."[18] A Mars Group works like this:

> "Imagine that you've been asked to recreate the very best attributes of your organization on another planet but you have seats on the rocket ship for only five to seven people. Whom should you send? Most likely, you'll choose the people who have a gut level understanding of your core values, the highest level of credibility with their peers, and the highest level of competence. We'll often ask people brought together to work on core values to nominate a Mars Group of five to seven people (not necessarily from the assembled group). Invariably they end up selecting highly credible representatives who do a super job of articulating the core values precisely because they are exemplars of those values—a representative slice of the company's genetic code."[19]

More than 2,000 years ago, Aristotle observed that if communication is to change behavior, it must be grounded in the desires and interests of those who receive it. Since 350 BC, there have been no major changes in that central idea.[20]

Training

Touching employee values means that, just like setting work objectives and conducting appraisals, the training needs to be in line with what will actually work. How much will the training count on an everyday basis? Are there supports in place to leverage the training? How will related growth and development be fostered once the PowerPoint presentation goes dark?

In *The Fifth Discipline*, Peter Senge wrote, "Organizations learn only through individuals who learn."[21] Yet many organizations offer little or no training when it comes to evaluating performance and conducting performance appraisal sessions. It often seems that firms believe promotion to a supervisory or managerial position automatically gives an individual the ability to perform all managerial functions, without formalized training. Most performance appraisal problems could be eliminated through proper training—training that begins with promotion to a supervisory position and is reinforced through at least annual updating sessions.[22]

Basic to any appraisal training are techniques for applying work standards and setting them jointly with employees. How to avoid rating errors should also be high on the list. Coaching and counseling skills based on directly observed behavior are equally essential to a solid training agenda. "'Management by wandering around,' a concept popularized by Tom Peters, is the tactic of observing what's occurring firsthand, and it's a good one. Mishandled—and it's easy to do—it often becomes 'management by stumbling around.'"[23]

Training in the performance system should be directed to both employees and managers, and it should be designed based on how adults learn. As quoted in an article for *Training/HRD Magazine*, adults will learn only what they feel a need to learn, seek to learn what they have identified as important, look to learning what can be immediately applied, and learn by doing.[24] Employees trained in performance appraisals become empowered to take charge of their own performance. They are better prepared to initiate discussions about their work and to do self-appraisals on a continuing basis. After participating in training, employees should be able to understand the process, monitor their own performance, be clear about the importance of taking responsibility for their work, accept feedback, and pursue their own professional development. They should benefit from understanding the importance of performance management in their organization and their particular role in bolstering it.

Retraining should occur each year. Be sure new employees and managers are introduced to the performance system early on. Don't forget to train those managers who were promoted from within the organization as well. Training is especially key when a new system is introduced. Benchmark and stay abreast of best practices, within the Human Resources field, tracking what's working at other organizations.

To receive consistent feedback is perhaps the biggest pay-off for the employee. Employees deserve to know where their talents are and how they can build more skills and develop professionally. Getting that feedback is a prime reason that employees stay with a company, surveys have shown.

Monitoring and Assessment

The most important job skill in this era of constant change is the ability to learn and relearn. But communicating and training are not necessarily agents of change. Just because they occur does not mean they are working. Even if they are working, the results may be short-lived. Is the pay-off immediate? Still going strong in a month? Six months? Do trainees exhibit a really fresh understanding? And if so, are they demonstrating it in new, desired ways, or is their performance basically unchanged?

The process is eased by top-quality hiring, in which a "good fit" upfront translates into eager, dedicated employee performance most of the time. But the communication and training are meant for current employees, so the aim is to make them work well and leverage the benefits as widely as possible. With performance appraisals, it's

Sound Appraisals

According to Robert H. Woods, to ensure sound appraisals, you must:

1. Understand rating errors.

2. Understand how to process observed information.

3. Understand how to establish a frame of reference for what is observed.

4. Be familiar with the performance appraisal system in use.

5. Experience observing a performance appraisal.

6. Practice effective interviewing techniques.

7. Practice conducting a performance appraisal.[25]

easier to gauge the effects of training than of some other initiatives designed to change behavior. Are supervisors making fewer rating errors? Are employees more engaged? Is talk about setting objectives livelier—even becoming a genuine debate? Are mini-reviews occurring more frequently, or perhaps for the first time?

To answer these questions, managers can use both observable behavior and their "gut barometer." It's important to stay tuned: investing in communications and training will be counterproductive if employee performance remains unchanged.

Feedback should be sought soon after the training or specific communications, and again at a later time. "In the study of human behavior psychologists discovered a long time ago that feedback is one of the most critical requirements for sustained high-level performance of any human act. Without frequent and specific feedback, performance varies and often fails."[26] Drucker says, "It has been estimated that approximately 50 percent of the nonperformance problems in business occur because of lack of feedback."[27] Even after receiving sound training or communications, workers need feedback about how they are demonstrating its effects.

Challenges as Evaluations Evolve

Envisioning how businesses in the then-coming century will be "seen, understood and managed entirely as an integrated process," Peter Drucker wrote, "manager[s] will have to acquire a whole new set of tools—many of which [they] will have to develop themselves. [They] will need to acquire adequate yardsticks for performance and results in the key areas of business objectives."[28] Drucker also pointed out that "the best and most dedicated people are ultimately volunteers."[29]

Indicating that as companies move forward, they will need to draw on the full creative energy and talent of their people, Collins and Porras asked "why people should give full measure." They arrived at a pair of questions to be asked of each staff member: "How could we frame the purpose of this organization so that if you woke up each morning with enough money to retire, you would nevertheless keep working here? What deeper sense of purpose would motivate you to continue to dedicate your precious creative energies to this company's efforts?"[30]

Globalization presents particular challenges for the future, including international companies' mix of different cultures and hiring or importing local staff. Add a queasy economy with RIFs to the workplace mix, and appraisals become even more vital. Conducted effectively, they are essential in clarifying organizational expectations, rewarding good performance, recognizing specific employee interests, and providing a predictable structure in an often tough, uncertain world.

Here are suggested approaches to handling some of the challenges of this new era:

Flextime

Because companies define flextime differently, it can be difficult to translate best practices from one organization to another. Many different arrangements are made to help employees maintain more balanced lives. For some companies, flextime involves building work hours around an identified core period when all employees are expected to be at the office or work location. Other employers allow major adjustments in an employee's weekly schedule with advance notice. Another model compresses hours into a shortened workweek.

The U.S. Bureau of Labor Statistics reported that in May 2004, more than 27 million full-time wage and salary workers had flexible work schedules that allowed them to vary the time they began or ended work.[31] A study by William M. Mercer of 800 firms with 1,000 or more employees found that 34 percent use compressed workweeks for some part of their workforce, and an additional 14 percent are considering this approach.[32]

Flextime appears to contribute to decreased tardiness, reduced absenteeism, less job fatigue, increased organizational loyalty, and improved recruitment.[33] It should not adversely affect the performance management process: objectives should be set and measured at regularly scheduled mini-reviews, and the employee must show a willingness to do quality work and make the new schedule operate predictably and seamlessly. To minimize problems, employees should stay organized and leave detailed directions for supervisors and co-workers, while being able to reach them when the unexpected occurs. They need to work at keeping each other in the loop. Because flextime often needs a "test run" to make sure it works, supervisors and employees can agree upfront on a time frame for it, after which the program can be adjusted or even discontinued—and discuss a schedule for performance review discussions.

Telecommuting

Telecommuting is here to stay. Whether it's instituted to save space at the office, increase employee retention, or just link work and home, it's usually a hit. The U.S. Department of Labor estimates that between 13 million and 19 million full-time or part-time employees telecommute.[34]

The International Telework Advisory Council identifies four factors necessary to make a telecommuting, or telework, program successful: dedicated resources, automated processes and technology, job function considerations, and manager characteristics. The manager should have above-average organizational, planning, and coaching skills; be able to focus on output rather than hours; be able to establish and evaluate well-defined, measurable objectives and goals; and provide timely and constructive feedback.[35] Managers should also be comfortable managing employees who are not in sight. Employees should be reliable, disciplined, and able to get work done with limited supervision. Good time management and communication skills really matter.

Consultant Yvonne Zhou, president of Futrend Technology Inc. in Virginia, says, "A teleworker must be evaluated as a non-teleworker. Telework forces managers to measure by performance, not by face time or the number of hours an employee is in the office."

Training managers and employees is critical to ensure good performance and high productivity among teleworkers and the success of a telework program. Managers need to learn how to manage, motivate, and collaborate with their telecommuting staff. As for all employees, managers must be shown how to develop clear performance standards and measures that evaluate an employee's performance based on objective criteria. The expectations must be discussed upfront. Employees should be self-disciplined and be able to handle varying situations. The supervisor and employee should agree to review the arrangement frequently and make changes or discontinue it as needed.

Job-Sharing

"There is a strong business case for job-sharing," says Honey Melville-Brown, a consultant who helped compile a study showing that "not only in terms of performance, but also as a critical retention tool, job-sharing is an excellent way to fill the skills gap. It may be a company's ideal to have a single, full-time person, but [companies] are realizing that it's better to have the right skills package spread across two bodies than an inadequate one in one."[36]

The challenge is to distribute tasks fairly and build strong communication between the job-sharers so that co-workers and customers aren't affected. Here, too, strong, measurable standards, consistent performance monitoring, and continuing, clear communication are key.

Performance evaluation in job-sharing is similar to evaluating part-time employees. Goal-setting is a major element. Responsibilities can be divided in ways that make sense and promote work continuity. Each worker's clear understanding of the objectives for which he or she is responsible ensures accountability.

Team Performance Appraisals

In evaluating the performance of a team, two assessments are needed: one for the entire team and one for each individual. Understanding and reinforcing the balance between them is important to the success of both, especially in organizations that value and promote teamwork. It takes motivated individuals to spur on the team. Many organizations now factor behaviors beneficial to team development into their criteria for individual performance. Employees are expected to deliver results in specific ways.

As Nelarine Cornelius states, "In a case study of self-managed groups at the Digital Equipment Corporation in Colorado Springs, Carol Norman and Robert Zwacki found that team appraisal appeared to improve participation, commitment, and productivity. The need to participate is reinforced by the requirement for all team members to take specific roles and responsibilities for performance appraisals."[37]

Yet a Mercer Management study found that just 13 of 179 teams received high ratings. "Somehow we need to get past this idea that all we have to do is join hands and sing 'Kumbaya' and say, 'We've moved to teamwork.' Many companies are narrowing the focus and horizon of teams."[38]

Virtual teams bring benefits along with complications. Just as with telecommuting, the supervisor's reliance on line-of-sight managing can create discomfort with this work arrangement.

Carl Worthy, an expert on off-site workers, explained, "Managers are process-focused. They think, 'I know you're doing a good job because I see you working.' Because that's impossible with virtual teams, managers have to focus on results. Managers also may find it difficult to coach and advise, assess training needs, and give feedback to team members who aren't in view. Reviews using 360-degree feedback can help managers understand how members are performing, and analyzing bulletin boards and intranets will give a feel for the team's issues and problems."[39]

Matrix Management

With appraisal issues similar to those of team evaluations, matrix management involves both horizontal and vertical reporting. Two or more intersecting lines of authority can run through the same individual, who typically reports to two supervisors. In matrix structures, the main or functional manager typically has primary responsibility for performance reviews, with matrix team leaders or product managers providing input.

Multiple Rater Appraisals and Multiple Supervisors

Various situations arise when there are multiple raters. For fairness and employee comfort, it is extremely important to be sure all on board are thoroughly grounded in what is being measured and whom is being evaluated; the employee should not feel as if this is a town meeting. Everyone's role should be clear to raters, supervisors, and the employee.

Just as in matrix management, it is usually the primary supervisor who takes the lead, with input from one or more supervisors who share management responsibility.

Goal-setting is crucial. All supervisors must agree on goals and the value or weight assigned to each goal. This establishes the priorities that will guide employee performance throughout the evaluation cycle. All supervisors should also commit to being available as needed to offer support and direction. Periodic mini-reviews are key to keeping everyone on the same track.

Upward Performance Appraisals

Mention employees reviewing managers, and managers often cringe. In part, upward appraisals are an extension of customer-focused thinking—those on the receiving end are best qualified to evaluate it. Today's employees don't want to be merely cogs in a wheel. They seek knowledge and understanding about their worlds and want to put that information to good use. Two-way evaluations often appeal to them.

Several challenges face an employer willing to give upward appraisals a shot. Should the employee/evaluators be anonymous? Anonymous evaluations are more likely to result in honest feedback. And how should the review be designed? The employee also needs to really know his or her supervisor's work firsthand—no long-distance speculation.

Though research has shown that supervisors do improve performance as a result of anonymous upward appraisals, it also shows, not surprisingly, that those who receive upward appraisals view non-anonymous feedback more positively. Conversely, employees view the process more positively when it is anonymous.[40] Managers who receive the appraisal and subsequent coaching are frequently the biggest supporters of the upward appraisal process.

This process requires employees to evaluate their supervisors on a set of pre-established criteria, often having to do with supervisory style and effectiveness. Any employer who wants to implement upward appraisals must be sure that evaluation criteria are unmistakably clear. It's best to pilot the process before launching it officially.

Sample Upward Appraisal

For each of the following statements, rate your supervisor on a scale of 1 to 5.

1 = Never does this.

2 = Does this sometimes.

3 = Does this about half the time.

4 = Does this most of the time.

5 = Always does this.

_____ 1. Really listens to me.

_____ 2. Delegates new assignments and the authority to oversee them.

_____ 3. Thoroughly explains projects.

_____ 4. Cares about my growth and development.

_____ 5. Encourages me to take risks.

_____ 6. Respects me.

_____ 7. Gives me credit on projects I've contributed to.

_____ 8. Creates a positive work setting.

_____ 9. Knows his/her job.

_____ 10. Supports my actions and decisions.

_____ 11. Asks for my input.

_____ 12. Treats all employees fairly.

_____ 13. Gives specific, timely feedback on an ongoing basis.

_____ 14. Motivates me.

_____ 15. Enforces policies equitably.

_____ 16. Is able to explain the organization's goals.

_____ 17. Helps me writes good, challenging objectives.

_____ 18. Keeps me informed of pertinent company information.

_____ 19. Is consistent.

_____ 20. Appreciates my efforts.[41]

360-Degree Feedback

360-Degree Feedback is an evaluation and feedback approach that comes from all directions—above, below, and all sides. Typically one employee is evaluated by the supervisor(s), peers, subordinates, customers, and possibly others. Also called Multi-Rater Feedback, this is the most comprehensive and costly form of performance review. It also provides the broadest range of employee performance feedback. It tends to consolidate peer evaluations, upward appraisals, and self-reviews. But because feedback comes from all directions, the approach carries the risks of rater bias and inconsistent focus. A manager, for example, may focus on results. Peers may focus on leadership potential or collegiality. Direct reports may look at whether they are included in decision-making.

Given the considerable cost and time, 360-degree appraisals can hurt more than they help, especially when performance measures stray from business objectives. They need to be administered for the right reasons, that is, in order to solve a problem or strengthen the value of an evaluation program. They can be useful to provide feedback for top management.

Again, it is important to be completely clear about expectations. Everyone participating should be knowledgeable about the process and trained in assessing behavior and performance without bias. Documenting is important. And decisions about how the information is to be used—for development purposes, to justify a raise or bonus, or some other objective—must be made early on, *before* the appraisal occurs. How the employee receives the feedback is another important training topic.

Automated Appraisals

The amount of time required to develop appraisals is criticized almost universally. Already overloaded with paperwork, managers and employees are not looking for more. The time-consuming nature of good appraisals is one reason why so many participants want to just get through them—fast.

One reason they take so long is the paper itself: writing, circulating, and keeping track of each form. Doing evaluations online can help. It's important that the organization know its goals, the features it wants to include, and the results it wants to draw from the process. To be effective, an evaluation software program should help manage and improve the paper-based process, not merely automate it.

Just automating a poor appraisal tool will not save time or simplify the process. It's still crucial to have clearly defined goals, performance standards that are understood and tied to the business plan, and action plans for dealing with any performance shortfalls. But once these elements are firmly in place, automating can make the process easier. A well-developed system can promote attention to training, performance gaps, and the need for course corrections. Training is essential to get the most out of the system.

Aging Workforce Is "Booming"

"Boomers want to problem-solve. Ask Nancy Boomer how she would handle XYZ if it arose in her workday."[42] Given that baby boomers are at or nearing retirement age, often with gaping holes in their savings, the workforce can benefit from millions of problem solvers. Indications are that large numbers of boomers aren't necessarily planning to retire at 65.

Raised with TV coverage of assassinations, Vietnam, and Watergate, boomers tend not to be as trusting as the previous generation, but theirs is a generation that continues to be vital, energetic, and involved. They can help organizations develop performance appraisals, structure a blueprint for the next evaluation cycle, build in victories along the way, and find ways to meet the challenges of this ever-changing era in the world of work.

Gen Xers

Although this generation is sometimes criticized for being self-focused and having a sense of "entitlement," a study commissioned by Deloitte & Touche and The Corporate State found that Gen Xers

Managing Gen Xers and Beyond

Generation X (born 1965–1976) 51 million

Mentoring Do's

✓ Casual, friendly work environment.
✓ Involvement.
✓ Flexibility and freedom.
✓ A place to learn.

Generation Y or Millenials (born 1977–1998) 75 million

Mentoring Do's

✓ Structured, supportive work environment.
✓ Personalized work.
✓ Interactive relationship.
✓ Be prepared for demands, high expectations.[44]

Source: The Learning Café and American Demographics Enterprising Museum 2003

want a work environment that is "stable" and "clearly structured."[43]

Margaret Lack, former principal and co-founder of The Millennium Group International, LLC in Virginia, wrote that "the key to Gen X appraisals is simple: Remember who the audience is!" She says Gen Xers place a high priority on self-reliance, independence, and work/life balance. They are goal-oriented and achievement-focused, meaning that their supervisors would be wise to develop a self-directed work environment, engaging the employee in targeting priorities and goals.

Because of this achievement orientation, it is important that Gen Xers see results, feel challenged, and learn new, marketable skills. As a rule, Gen Xers will want coaching. The ongoing nature of performance management will be appealing. Gen Xers tend to be flexible and technologically savvy; they often "think outside the box." Lack advised customizing the appraisal process, with collaborative goal-setting to address self-management and achievement needs. Goals can be developed with continuing milestones so that Gen X employees can experience results early and often. "Stretch goals" can be tailored to particular challenges—this is a generation that was raised on games. Coaching, mentoring, and frequent, fast feedback will add value to their work experience, Lack wrote.

Generation Y

Generation Y is "up for any challenge ('bring it on' may well be the motto), and they have an astonishing amount of expertise in technology....They work well in team environments," wrote Joanne Sujansky in *Workforce Magazine*. Generation Y will number 80 million, and their considerable volume makes retaining them a top priority for today's businesses.[45]

Sujansky wrote that members of Generation Y—also called The Millennials, among other labels—"live to be trained" and want to be asked for "their ideas and contributions." They should be given "opportunities to move up.... They want to know how their work fits into a company's big picture." Employers should make sure that corrective feedback is balanced with praise.

> ## Welcoming Generation Y
>
> ✓ Communicate the big picture.
> ✓ Motivate team-building.
> ✓ Create "cool" work assignments.
> ✓ Invite ideas.
> ✓ Balance correction with praise.

"Catch them doing something right, and reward them when you do… [they] absolutely thrive on recognition."[46] Generation Y will look for work assignments that are not just standard fare.

Eric Chester, an active speaker on "Generation Why," observed that Generation Y is "better educated, more creative and far more techno-savvy than those who have come before them. Employers can expect them to refuse to blindly conform to traditional standards and time-honored institutions."[47]

An important point concerning performance reviews is that there's no cookie-cutter approach to dealing with employees. Marcus Buckingham and Curt Coffman say in their book *First Break All the Rules* that we don't breathe the same psychological oxygen.

So get to know your employees and tailor your message—either positive reinforcement or gentle redirection—to each one. Do all you can to create an environment that motivates and engages them.

Appendix

Sample Forms

Note: All forms included in this appendix are *samples only*. In light of changing legal requirements and state law variations, employers should always consult with employment counsel before using them.

Sample Performance Appraisal Form #1

Used by permission of Atlantic Human Resource Advisors, LLC.

EMPLOYEE PERFORMANCE REVIEW

Employee Name : _____

Position Title: _____

Department#: _____ Date of Hire: _____ In Current Job Since: _____

Due in HR:_____ Effective Date: _____

Performance Factors

1. Job Knowledge				
Has poor knowledge of job; requires ongoing training instruction and direction.	Has fair knowledge and comprehension of job; requires minimum direction in completing work.	Has sufficient knowledge and comprehension of job; requires minimum direction in completing work.	Has thorough knowledge and comprehension of job; rarely requires additional direction.	Has excellent knowledge and comprehension of job; works independently.
6	12	18	24	30

2. Decision-Making				
Unable to make decisions is unacceptable, does not take initiative.	Decision-making barely meets minimum standards.	Takes initiative to make average decisions.	Can make decisions that exceed standards.	Consistently takes initiative to make effective decisions.
6	12	18	24	30

3. Quality of Work				
Work quality is unacceptable; causes and/or creates an excessive number of errors.	Work quality barely meets minimum standards; error rate is high.	Work quality meets job standards; error rate is acceptable.	Work quality exceeds acceptable standards; rarely makes errors; shows pride in work.	Consistently produces accurate and quality work; always shows pride in work.
6	12	18	24	30

4.	Quantity of Work			
Works at an extremely slow pace; produces an unacceptable volume of work. **6**	Works at a slow pace; volume of work falls short of requirements. **12**	Works at a steady pace; produces an acceptable volume of work. **18**	Works at a fast pace; exceeds acceptable requirements; often produces a large volume of work. **24**	Works at a rapid pace; consistently produces a large volume of work. **30**

5.	Human Relations			
Discourteous or abrupt with team and other employees; unconcerned about the needs of others. Does not praise team. **5**	Occasionally abrupt when dealing with peers and team; somewhat indifferent to the needs of others. **10**	Normally pleasant and courteous to the team and employees; lends assistance when needed. **15**	Consistently courteous and helpful to customers and employees. **20**	Demonstrates outstanding interpersonal relations with peers and employees; Recognizes and praises team members/ peers for their efforts. **25**

6.	Attendance/Punctuality			
Excessively absent or tardy; attendance record not acceptable. **5**	Frequently absent or tardy; barely acceptable attendance record. **10**	Occasionally absent or tardy; attendance record acceptable. **15**	Seldom absent or tardy; dependable. **20**	Excellent attendance record; rarely absent or tardy; very dependable. **25**

7.	Initiative			
Needs constant prodding to complete work; no enthusiasm; deadlines are constantly missed. **4**	Needs some prodding to complete work; shows little enthusiasm; deadlines are occasionally missed. **8**	Routine worker; accepts additional tasks when asked; seldom seeks new tasks. **12**	Handles assignments efficiently and timely; usually willing to accept or seek new assignments. **6**	Displays confidence and enthusiasm in accepting or seeking new assignments; assists others voluntarily. **20**

8.   Organization of Work

Work is constantly disorganized, resulting in major workflow disruption.	Work is usually disorganized, resulting in minor workflow disruption.	Work is usually organized, resulting in acceptable workflow.	Work is always organized, resulting in smooth workflow.	Work is always extremely organized, resulting in most efficient workflow.
4	8	12	16	20

9.   Adaptability

Is unable or unwilling to learn news tasks; resists change.	Learns new tasks slowly and reluctantly; has some difficulty accepting change.	Adapts to and learns new tasks at normal speed; usually willing to accept change.	Learns new tasks quickly and easily; accepts change with minimum difficulty.	Exceptionally quick at learning new tasks; handles assignments easily; very flexible to change.
3	6	9	12	15

10.   Acceptance of Feedback

Becomes very defensive when given constructive feedback; places blame, gets angry and/or makes excuses.	Becomes defensive at times when given constructive feedback; occasionally makes excuses, becomes angry or places blame.	Generally accepts constructive feedback well.	Consistently accepts constructive feedback well.	Clearly and consistently accepts feedback exceptionally well; sees feedback as a way to learn.
3	6	9	12	15

11.   Communication

Has poor verbal and/or written communication skills.	Has fair verbal and/or written communication skills.	Has sufficient verbal and written communication skills.	Has very good verbal and written communication skills.	Has exceptional verbal and written communication skills.
3	6	9	12	15

12. Management/Supervision

Has poor supervisory skills; requires ongoing training, instruction and direction; is not always honest/fair when dealing others; rarely provides constructive feedback to subordinates.	Has fair supervisory skills; requires more than normal amount of instruction/direction; is usually honest/fair when dealing others; sometimes provides constructive feedback to subordinates.	Has sufficient supervisory skills; requires minimum direction; consistently honest/fair when dealing with others; generally provides constructive feedback to subordinates.	Has very good supervisory skills; rarely requires additional assistance in managing departmental issues; consistently provides constructive feedback to subordinates.	Has excellent supervisory skills; work well independently in managing departmental issues; always provides constructive feedback to subordinates.
3	6	9	12	15

Performance Factors	1	2	3	4	5	6	7	8	9	10	11	12	13	Total Points
Points														

*Please Note: Only calculate the points in #13 when reviewing non-exempt supervisors.

Below Standard (51-74 Points)	Fair (75-128 Points)	Competent (129-179 Points)	Commendable (180-230 Points)	Distinguished (231-255 Points)

*Use this Points Scale when calculating points for Performance Factors 1 through 12

Below Standard (54-78 Points)	**Fair (79-135 Points)**	**Competent (136-189 Points)**	**Commendable (190-243 Points)**	**Distinguished (244-270 Points)**
*Use this Points Scale when calculating points for Performance Factors 1 through 13				

Indicate any additional comments that support the performance rating on this form:

_____

_____

_____

Summarize the employee's job-related strengths:

_____

_____

_____

Summarize the employee's job-related weaknesses, and provide recommendations for improvement:

_____

_____

_____

Indicate specific goals or actions planned for the next performance review period:

_____

_____

_____

REQUIRED SIGNATURES

The completed form must be signed by the Employee and Manager/Director. The completed form should be returned to the Human Resources Department, where the rating will be recorded and the form filed in the employee's personnel file.

Employee's Comments:

_____

_____

_____

I acknowledge having read this Performance Review.

Employee Signature: _____ Date: _____

Manager/Director's Comments:

_____

_____

_____

Manager/Director's Signature: _____ Date: _____

Sample Performance Appraisal Form #2

Used by permission of the National Council of La Raza.

Performance Evaluation Form

Employee:	Title:	
Component:	Supervisor:	
Date of Hire:	Date of Last Evaluation:	Time Period of This Evaluation:
Evaluation Type: 90-Day Annual Other *(explain)*		

Instructions

- This form is used to evaluate the employee's performance and to record that evaluation for use by the organization. The employee's performance should be evaluated against specific expectations of key responsibilities or standards of the job.

- The employee's supervisor must complete and review with the next level of management.

- The evaluation should be discussed with employee. The employee should complete the "Comment" section (see page 6), if applicable. Employee and supervisor must sign the form in designated spaces when completed.

- Completed form should be submitted to Human Resources Department, with one copy to employee and one to supervisor.

Standards and Competency

A set of core NCLR competencies is listed. You may include core standards from the job description, component, or department goals. You may also include additional competencies related to your component/department. The rating scale is **1 to 5.**

1	Unsatisfactory: the lowest rating, which means that performance is consistently below the accepted standard or that the employee did not meet the goal on time or within other prescribed limits
2	Needs Improvement: performance quality and/or quantity is inconsistent, at times requiring additional work
3	Satisfactory: the accepted standard of performance or behavior
4	Exemplary Performance: consistently above average
5	Excellent: the highest level of performance, consistently above the standard

Description of Competency and/or Standards From the Job Description or Component	Rating	Comments
Technical Knowledge: Is fully capable of using all available technologies that positively impact the work, goals, and mission. Has the substantive knowledge to perform current job functions.		
Quality of Work: Meets NCLR standard of work; work is submitted error-free the first time. Is committed to continuous improvement; is open to suggestions, creating an environment leading to the most efficient and effective work processes.		

Description of <u>Competency</u> and/or <u>Standards</u> From the Job Description or Component	Rating	Comments
Timely Work: Consistently sets and meets time lines; works in coordination with other staff to ensure time lines are met; renegotiates deadlines at earliest point at which original plan is in jeopardy. Manages workload and delivers the product promised. Understands direction, clarifies as needed.		
Communication Skills: Proficient writing and oral skills both for internal and external communications. Is easy to approach and talk to; builds rapport well; is a good listener; is effective in presenting (if applicable) in formal and informal settings.		
Initiative: Takes charge of tasks at hand with minimal need for guidance and acts appropriately; understands the "Big Picture" and makes it happen.		
Strategic Ability: Sees ahead clearly; can anticipate future consequences and trends accurately; can paint credible visions of possibilities and likelihoods. Anticipates needs and plans ahead. Is a problem-solver.		

Description of <u>Competency</u> and/or <u>Standards</u> From the Job Description or Component	Rating	Comments
Decision-Making Abilities: Exercises sound judgment, analysis, wisdom, and experience confidently and assertively. Makes decisions in a timely manner based on available information and within tight deadlines and pressures.		
Teamwork: Integrates into teams, encourages collaboration, and is capable of creating strong morale through sharing of wins and successes; fosters open dialogue; defines success in terms of the whole team and creates feeling of belonging in the team.		
Achieves Impact: Understands goals and objectives, both personal and organizational, and pursues them to completion; sees clear connection between mission, goals, and personal results. Can differentiate and prioritize tasks based on relevance to desired impact.		
Rate the following, if applicable; add additional competencies or standards as applicable to the specific position.		
Leadership Skills: Develops strategies that advance work/ employee development and overall institutional goals. Learns from and shares with others. Creates a positive work environment. Inspires and focuses on possibilities.		

Description of <u>Competency</u> and/or <u>Standards</u> From the Job Description or Component	Rating	Comments

<u>Goals and Overall Performance From Last Year</u>

List goals/objectives based on the individual's program plan or from the individual's previous performance evaluation.

Goals/Objectives	Rating	Comments

Overall Performance	Rating	Comments
To what extent did individual's work consistently meet requirements/objectives of work plan?		
Identify major accomplishments achieved.		
Note objectives not achieved.		

<u>Goals for Next Performance Cycle</u>

Based on the goals of NCLR, or your component, list those for which you will have primary responsibility and the timetable for completion.

Goals	Timetable

<u>Development Plan for Next Performance Cycle</u>

Skills/ Knowledge/ Experience	Actions	Timetable
Strengths: • What key strengths could employee leverage/build on to increase future effectiveness? • What effective behavior should employee continue to use in managing or working with others?		
Areas for Improvement: • What skills can be strengthened to enhance effectiveness, progress, and career goals? • What should the employee start or stop doing to be more effective?		

Supervisor Comments/Recommendations

_____

_____

_____

Supervisor Signature: _____ Date: _____

Employee Comments

_____

_____

_____

My signature means I have reviewed the evaluation and discussed the contents with my supervisor; it does not necessarily imply that I agree with this evaluation.

Employee Signature: _____ Date: _____

Forward completed and signed copy to HR Department and employee.

Sample Performance Appraisal Form #3

Used by permission of the Special Olympics.

Performance Review Form

Instructions for completing form:

1. Employee completes the self-assessment portions of the review (Sections 1-2) and submits to his/her supervisor by an agreed upon date.

2. The supervisor then completes his/her portion of the assessment (Section 3).

3. Once done, the supervisor schedules and holds a meeting with the employee to review and discuss performance and to hold an initial conversation about the employee's development goals.

4. Before a final overall rating is assigned to each employee, a calibration session will be held with supervisors to ensure ratings are applied consistently across departments. At the conclusion of this process, a final rating will be assigned to the employee (Section 4). At this time, the supervisor and employee should discuss and finalize a development plan (Section 6).

5. The employee will then have the opportunity to make any additional comments before signing the form (Section 5,7). The form should also be signed by the employee's supervisor and turned into HR for signature.

Section 1 - Employee Information

Employee Name: Current Supervisor:

Title: Dept:

Performance Period: Jan 1, 2008 – Dec 31, 2008

Section 2 - Employee Self-Assessment

Part 1: Employee provides a narrative assessment of overall performance during the review period, using examples of noteworthy accomplishments and of the impact of his/her work.

Part 2: Employee lists performance goals for the review period, and assesses performance against goals.

Note: Comments may be added to explain performance which exceeded or did not meet established goals. Comments may also be added to indicate changes in goals over the course of the review period, or external factors that impacted performance toward goals, such as new priorities, reduced resources, or other factors.

Clearly Above Average		Solid Performance	Needs Improvement				
F=Far Exceeded Goals	E= Exceeded Goals	M= Met Goals	P= Partially Met Goals	U= Unsatisfactory Performance			
				F	E	M	P	U
List Goal 1— COMMENTS:								
List Goal 2— COMMENTS:								
List Goal 3— COMMENTS:								
List Goal 4— COMMENTS:								
List Goal 5— COMMENTS:								

Section 3 – Supervisor Assessment

Part 1: The supervisor provides a detailed description of the employee's performance against assigned performance goals and provides examples to support assessment.

[ ]

Part 2: The supervisor rates the employee's performance in the following areas and provides examples to support rating.

Clearly Above Average		Solid Performance	Needs Improvement	
F=Far Exceed Expectations	E= Exceeds Expectations	M= Meets Expectations	P= Partially Meets Expectations	U= Unsatisfactory Performance
This Section Is To Be Completed For All Employees			F E M	P U

	F	E	M	P	U
JOB KNOWLEDGE—Competent in required job skills, is knowledgeable of the duties, methods, equipment, and procedures required by the job, displays understanding of how job relates to others, able to perform a wide variety of job-related tasks. COMMENTS:					
QUALITY OF WORK——Completes assignments in a thorough and accurate manner, produces quality work and achieves results under established quality standards. COMMENTS:					
INITIATIVE—Persistent and resilient in the pursuit of the assigned performance objects and goals COMMENTS:					
TEAMWORK—Demonstrates ability to get along with others, communicates and acts as a team player. COMMENTS:					
WORK ETHICS/HABITS—Demonstrates commitment and dedication to accomplishing assigned duties, has solid attendance record, arrives to work on time. COMMENTS:					

SERVICE QUALITY—Effectiveness in servicing both external and internal constituent/customers, responsive to constituent/customers, and meets constituent/customer expectations. COMMENTS:					
COMMUNICATION—Handles internal and/or external communications effectively, expresses ideas clearly in oral and written form, COMMENTS:					
This Section Is To Be Completed For Employees In A Supervisory Position	F	E	M	P	U
LEADERSHIP AND DIRECTION—Successfully coaches and mentors subordinates, clearly communicates goals for the work group, motivates others to perform well. COMMENTS:					
STRATEGY—Recommends, sets, implements, and communicates company and departmental goals/strategies and ability to move employees in that direction. COMMENTS:					
PLANNING/ORGANIZATION ABILITY—Sets goals and objectives of self and others, initiates and implements changes smoothly, plans and performs work systematically to meet stated objectives and priorities for self and subordinates COMMENTS:					
JUDGEMENT/DECISION-MAKING—Makes timely decisions and actions based on sound reasoning and weighing of outcomes, effective handling of sensitive matters, exhibits sound and accurate judgment, includes appropriate people in decision-making process COMMENTS:					

Section 4 – Performance Summary and Overall Rating

After the calibration process has been concluded, supervisor should check the appropriate box below. Rating should reflect the employee's total contribution, taking into consideration all comments and ratings assigned in Sections 2-3.

☐	Far Exceeds Expectations. <ul><li>Employee currently exceeds overall performance expectations for his/her position as outlined in Section 2, including aggressive, difficult, and complex objectives.</li><li>Employee consistently performs at an exceptional level well above the norm of what is expected, clearly setting him/her apart from peers.</li><li>Employee's results add significant value to the team, to Special Olympics, and its constituents.</li><li>Employee excels in demonstrating core competencies outlined in Section 3 and acts as a role model for other employees.</li></ul>
☐	Exceeds Expectations. <ul><li>Employee currently meets overall performance expectations for his/her position as outlined in Section 2, and exceeds many.</li><li>Employee consistently performs above the norm of what is expected for his/her position.</li><li>Employee's results add value to the team, to Special Olympics, and its constituents.</li><li>Employee performs above the norm in demonstrating core competencies outlined in Section 3.</li></ul>
☐	Meets Expectations. <ul><li>Employee currently meets all or most of the performance expectations for their position, as outlined in Section 2.</li><li>Employee's results add value to the team, to Special Olympics, and its constituents.</li><li>Employee fully demonstrates the core competencies outlined in Section 3.</li></ul>

☐	Partially Meets Expectations. • Employee sometimes meets agreed upon results, but does not meet all expectations as outlined in Section 2. • Employee demonstrates some of the core competencies outlined in Section 3, but does not demonstrate all of them consistently. • Employee requires immediate attention to performance improvement to meet the expected performance level.
☐	Unsatisfactory. • Employees in this category are currently unsatisfactory and require immediate performance improvement to continue in their position.

Section 5 – Additional Employee Comments (Optional)

This section is to be used for any additional comments the employee wishes to make concerning the appraisal.

Section 6 – Development Plan

Employee and his/her supervisor should consider performance in the review period, as well as performance goals set for the coming year, and discuss development needs to enhance performance or help employee meet new goals. Employee and his/her supervisor should also discuss employee's career development goals over the next 3-5 years, such as new areas of responsibility and vertical or lateral movement within the organization. The development plan below should reflect both the interests and goals of the employee and the needs of Special Olympics.

Development Resources			
• Continuing Education • Job Cross-Training • Inter-departmental work • Project Management	• Computer based Training • Project Assignments • Professional Certification • Supervisory Training	• Professional Seminars • Professional Associations • Coaching • Regional/Program experience	• Mentoring • On-the-job Training • Publications/Presentations

Development Focus	Actions Planned	Status/Timing

Section 7 – Signatures

I have reviewed and discussed this Performance Assessment and Development Plan with my Supervisor and have been advised of the assessment level of my performance. My signature below does not imply my agreement with the performance assessment, but rather indicates that the discussion took place and that I was afforded the opportunity to record additional comments, if I so desired.

Employee_____ Date _____
            Print name   Signature

Supervisor _____ Date _____
            Print name   Signature

HR Representative _____ Date _____
            Print name   Signature

Sample Performance Appraisal Form #4

Used by permission of the Folcomer Equipment Corporation.

Performance Evaluation Form

Employee name: _____

Date: _____

Person conducting review: _____

Score the performance in each job factor below on a scale of 1-5, as follows:

5 = Outstanding, consistently exceeds expectations and is recognized by peers and/or customers as a leader and positive example for others.

4 = Above Expectations, consistently meets and occasionally exceeds expectations.

3 = Meets Expectations, consistently meets expectations.

2 = Below Expectations, occasionally fails to meet expectations.

1 = Needs Improvement, consistently fails to meet expectations and a job performance improvement plan is required.

Job factor	Employee Self-Evaluation	Manager Evaluation	Comments
Job-specific knowledge			
Quality of work			
Quantity of work			
Dependability			
Punctuality and attendance			
Interpersonal/ communication skills			
Teamwork			
Customer service			
Other (please specify):			

Additional comments:

_____

_____

Goals for next review period/areas for improvement:

_____

_____

Signatures

Employee: _____ Date: _____

Manager: _____ Date: _____

Human Resources: _____ Date: _____

Sample Performance Appraisal Form #5

Used by permission of the National Association of Federal Credit Unions.

Cover Sheet

Employee Name:	
Reviewer:	
Date Completed:	

2009 Performance Evaluation

Title:	
Years in Position:	
Review Start Date:	
Review End Date:	

☐ Position Description Reviewed/Updated

Reviews

Interim 01 Date:	
Interim 02 Date:	
Self Eval Date:	
Date Due to HR:	

Employee Name:	
Reviewer:	
Date Completed:	

<u>**Section A**</u>
Performance Factors

2009 Performance Evaluation

1. **Job Knowledge & Application**	Rating of Expectations ○ Far Exceeds ○ Exceeds ○ Successfully Meets ○ Partially Meets ○ Does Not Meet
	Comments:
Rate the employee's technical knowledge and skills; analytical abilities, and problem-solving skills.	Type over the example text and enter your comments about the employee here. Your comments should reflect the accomplishments noted in the employee's self-evaluation form and rate the employee's performance against the expectations in these standard performance factors.
2. **Organization & Quality of work**	Rating of Expectations ○ Far Exceeds ○ Exceeds ○ Successfully Meets ○ Partially Meets ○ Does Not Meet
	Comments:
Rate the employee's accuracy, neatness, thoroughness, and completeness of work.	Type over the example text and enter your comments about the employee here. Your comments should reflect the accomplishments noted in the employee's self-evaluation form and rate the employee's performance against the expectations in these standard performance factors.
3. **Time Management & Productivity**	Rating of Expectations ○ Far Exceeds ○ Exceeds ○ Successfully Meets ○ Partially Meets ○ Does Not Meet
	Comments:
Rate the employee's work output, speed, timeliness, effectiveness, and work habits. Also assess performance in meeting deadlines.	Type over the example text and enter your comments about the employee here. Your comments should reflect the accomplishments noted in the employee's self-evaluation form and rate the employee's performance against the expectations in these standard performance factors.

4. **Interpersonal Skills & Teamwork**	Rating of Expectations ○ Far Exceeds ○ Exceeds ○ Successfully Meets ○ Partially Meets ○ Does Not Meet
	Comments:
Rate the employee's working relationships, teamwork, conflict resolution, and cooperation.	Type over the example text and enter your comments about the employee here. Your comments should reflect the accomplishments noted in the employee's self-evaluation form and rate the employee's performance against the expectations in these standard performance factors.
5. **Problem-Solving & Judgment**	Rating of Expectations ○ Far Exceeds ○ Exceeds ○ Successfully Meets ○ Partially Meets ○ Does Not Meet
	Comments:
Rate the employee's use of logical and sound judgement.	Type over the example text and enter your comments about the employee here. Your comments should reflect the accomplishments noted in the employee's self-evaluation form and rate the employee's performance against the expectations in these standard performance factors.
6. **Communication**	Rating of Expectations ○ Far Exceeds ○ Exceeds ○ Successfully Meets ○ Partially Meets ○ Does Not Meet
	Comments:
Rate the employee's written and verbal communication, presentation skills, and listening skills.	Type over the example text and enter your comments about the employee here. Your comments should reflect the accomplishments noted in the employee's self-evaluation form and rate the employee's performance against the expectations in these standard performance factors.
7. **Resource Management**	Rating of Expectations ○ Far Exceeds ○ Exceeds ○ Successfully Meets ○ Partially Meets ○ Does Not Meet
	Comments:
Rate the manager's budgeting and financial management skills, effective use of resources, and use of technology tools.	Type over the example text and enter your comments about the employee here. Your comments should reflect the accomplishments noted in the employee's self-evaluation form and rate the employee's performance against the expectations in these standard performance factors.

8. **Leadership & Management**	Rating of Expectations
	○ Far Exceeds ○ Exceeds ○ Successfully Meets
	○ Partially Meets ○ Does Not Meet
	Comments:
Rate the manager's skill in coaching, motivating, supervising, decision-making; as well as communication with and development of employees, and serving as a role model.	Type over the example text and enter your comments about the employee here. Your comments should reflect the accomplishments noted in the employee's self-evaluation form and rate the employee's performance against the expectations in these standard performance factors.

Employee Name:			**Section B**
Reviewer:			Annual Goals
Date Completed:			

2009 Performance Evaluation

GOAL 1	Rating of Expectations
	○ Far Exceeds ○ Exceeds ○ Successfully Meets
	○ Partially Meets ○ Does Not Meet
	Comments:
Enter Goal 1.	Type over the example text and enter your comments about the employee's accomplishment of the goal here. Your comments should reflect accomplishments noted in the employee's self-evaluation form and rate the employee's performance against the specific and measureable language in the goals established for the review year.

GOAL 2	Rating of Expectations
	○ Far Exceeds ○ Exceeds ○ Successfully Meets
	○ Partially Meets ○ Does Not Meet
	Comments:
Enter Goal 2.	Type over the example text and enter your comments about the employee's accomplishment of the goal here. Your comments should reflect accomplishments noted in the employee's self-evaluation form and rate the employee's performance against the specific and measureable language in the goals established for the review year.

GOAL 3	Rating of Expectations ○ Far Exceeds ○ Exceeds ○ Successfully Meets ○ Partially Meets ○ Does Not Meet
Enter Goal 3.	**Comments:**
	Type over the example text and enter your comments about the employee's accomplishment of the goal here. Your comments should reflect accomplishments noted in the employee's self-evaluation form and rate the employee's performance against the specific and measureable language in the goals established for the review year.

GOAL 4	Rating of Expectations ○ Far Exceeds ○ Exceeds ○ Successfully Meets ○ Partially Meets ○ Does Not Meet
Enter Goal 4.	**Comments:**
	Type over the example text and enter your comments about the employee's accomplishment of the goal here. Your comments should reflect accomplishments noted in the employee's self-evaluation form and rate the employee's performance against the specific and measureable language in the goals established for the review year.

GOAL 5	Rating of Expectations ○ Far Exceeds ○ Exceeds ○ Successfully Meets ○ Partially Meets ○ Does Not Meet
Enter Goal 5.	**Comments:**
	Type over the example text and enter your comments about the employee's accomplishment of the goal here. Your comments should reflect accomplishments noted in the employee's self-evaluation form and rate the employee's performance against the specific and measureable language in the goals established for the review year.

GOAL 6	Rating of Expectations ○ Far Exceeds ○ Exceeds ○ Successfully Meets ○ Partially Meets ○ Does Not Meett
Enter Goal 6.	**Comments:**
	Type over the example text and enter your comments about the employee's accomplishment of the goal here. Your comments should reflect accomplishments noted in the employee's self-evaluation form and rate the employee's performance against the specific and measureable language in the goals established for the review year.

GOAL 7	Rating of Expectations ○ Far Exceeds ○ Exceeds ○ Successfully Meets ○ Partially Meets ○ Does Not Meetot Meet
Enter Goal 7.	**Comments:**
	Type over the example text and enter your comments about the employee's accomplishment of the goal here. Your comments should reflect accomplishments noted in the employee's self-evaluation form and rate the employee's performance against the specific and measureable language in the goals established for the review year.

GOAL 8	Rating of Expectations ○ Far Exceeds ○ Exceeds ○ Successfully Meets ○ Partially Meets ○ Does Not Meet
Enter Goal 8.	**Comments:**
	Type over the example text and enter your comments about the employee's accomplishment of the goal here. Your comments should reflect accomplishments noted in the employee's self-evaluation form and rate the employee's performance against the specific and measureable language in the goals established for the review year.

Employee Name:	
Reviewer:	
Date Completed:	

2009 Performance Evaluation

Section C
Summary Page

Performance Factors	Total	Weight (%)	Rating
1. Job Knowledge/Application	0	**0.0%**	0
2. Organization/Quality of Work	0	**0.0%**	0
3. Time Management/Productivity	0	**0.0%**	0
4. Interpersonal Skills/Teamwork	0	**0.0%**	0
5. Problem Solving/Judgment	0	**0.0%**	0
6. Communication	0	**0.0%**	0
7. Resource Management	0	**0.0%**	0
8. Leadership/Management	0	**0.0%**	0
AVERAGE	**0.00**		

Annual Goals	Total	Weight (%)	Rating
Goal 1	0	**0.0%**	0
Goal 2	0	**0.0%**	0
Goal 3	0	**0.0%**	0
Goal 4	0	**0.0%**	0
Goal 5	0	**0.0%**	0
Goal 6	0	**0.0%**	0
Goal 7	0	**0.0%**	0
Goal 8	0	**0.0%**	0
0.00			

SCALE

Far Exceeds
4.60 – 5.00
Exceeds
3.60 – 4.59
Succ. Meets
3.86 – 3.59
Partially Meets
2.20 – 2.85
Does Not Meet
1.00 – 2.19

**TOTAL
REVIEW
SCORE**

0.00

Employee Name:	
Reviewer:	
Date Completed:	

2009 Performance Evaluation

Goals for 2010

GOAL 1	Comments:
Enter Goal 1 – concentrate on establishing specific, measurable, and attainable goals.	During the year, type over this example text and note ongoing progress toward your goal here.

GOAL 2	Comments:
Enter Goal 2 – concentrate on establishing specific, measurable, and attainable goals.	During the year, type over this example text and note ongoing progress toward your goal here.

GOAL 3	Comments:
Enter Goal 3 – concentrate on establishing specific, measurable, and attainable goals.	During the year, type over this example text and note ongoing progress toward your goal here.

GOAL 4	Comments:
Enter Goal 4 – concentrate on establishing specific, measurable, and attainable goals.	During the year, type over this example text and note ongoing progress toward your goal here.

GOAL 5	Comments:
Enter Goal 5 – concentrate on establishing specific, measurable, and attainable goals.	During the year, type over this example text and note ongoing progress toward your goal here.

GOAL 6	Comments:
Enter Goal 6 – concentrate on establishing specific, measurable, and attainable goals.	During the year, type over this example text and note ongoing progress toward your goal here.

GOAL 7	Comments:
Enter Goal 7 – concentrate on establishing specific, measurable, and attainable goals.	During the year, type over this example text and note ongoing progress toward your goal here.

GOAL 8	Comments:
Enter Goal 8 – concentrate on establishing specific, measurable, and attainable goals.	During the year, type over this example text and note ongoing progress toward your goal here.

Employee Name:	
Reviewer:	
Date Completed:	

2009 Performance Evaluation

Section D
Comments/Signatures

Reviewer's Comments	**Comments:**
Enter summary comments as the Reviewer...	Type over the example text and enter your comments about the employee here. Your comments should reflect the accomplishments and goals, and should be completed prior to discussing the review with the employee.

Reviewee's Comments	**Comments:**
Enter summary comments as the Reviewee...	Copy comments provided by the employee and paste them in this text box. The employee should be allowed a reasonable amount of time to complete comments that are provided in this annual review document.

Signatures			
Reviewer:		**Date:**	
Reviewee:		**Date:**	
Dept VP (if different from Reviewer):		**Date:**	
Director of HR:		**Date:**	

Sample Performance Appraisal Form #6

Used by permission of a DC-based association.

PERFORMANCE PLAN & REVIEW
Annual Review Form

Associate's Name: _____

Position: _____

Supervisor's Name: _____

Review Date: _____

Department: _____

Date Sent to Human Resources: _____

<u>Performance Rating Definitions</u>
<u>Performance consistently and significantly exceeds expectations and position requirements</u>

Performance which is clearly exceptional. Performance consistently surpasses all expectations for the job. The associate consistently exceeds an above average level of performance. This level of performance indicates the capability of assuming new responsibilities within a larger framework and eligibility for promotion. Performance reflects competence, dependability at all times and the capability to succeed in all tasks with a great degree of autonomy. Little or no supervision is required. Activities always contribute to improved or innovative work practices. This category applies to truly outstanding performers—those who serve as role models for others.

Performance consistently meets and sometimes exceeds expectations and position requirements.

Performance which provides a contribution that exceeds the defined expectations of the job. The associate regularly accomplishes more than is required and is capable of identifying problems, providing solutions and taking full responsibility for the results. Little supervision is needed. Associate at this level consistently does the work that is required. This category is for associates who are solid performers and competent at all aspects of their job.

Performance consistently meets expectations and position requirements.

Performance is entirely acceptable. Quality of work corresponds to the job requirements. Employee achieves the objectives set. Work is performed with a minimum of difficulty and error.

Performance meets some but not all expectations and position requirements.

Performance does not entirely meet job requirements. Not all objectives have been reached. Improvement is needed in certain areas. This rating may be given due to brief tenure in position, creating the requirement for more time to fulfill performance expectations. Supervision is required.

Performance does not meet expectations and position requirements.

Performance does not meet expectations for the job. This category includes associates who must demonstrate immediate improvement. Corrective action is necessary.

Section 1: Key Job Responsibilities

List three to six parts of the job that require the most time, attention and effort and, for each responsibility, identify specific objectives to be achieved. Rate the associate's performance in each area and provide comments and examples to support the rating.

Responsibility:
Specific Objectives:
Comments:

❏ Consistently & Significantly Exceeds Expectations & Position Requirements
❏ Consistently Meets & Sometimes Exceeds Expectations & Position Requirements
❏ Consistently Meets Expectations & Position Requirements
❏ Meets Some but not all Expectations & Position Requirements
❏ Does not meet Expectations & Position Requirements

Responsibility:
Specific Objectives:
Comments:

❏ Consistently & Significantly Exceeds Expectations & Position Requirements
❏ Consistently Meets & Sometimes Exceeds Expectations & Position Requirements
❏ Consistently Meets Expectations & Position Requirements
❏ Meets Some but not all Expectations & Position Requirements
❏ Does not meet Expectations & Position Requirements

Responsibility:
Specific Objectives:
Comments:

❏ Consistently & Significantly Exceeds Expectations & Position Requirements
❏ Consistently Meets & Sometimes Exceeds Expectations & Position Requirements
❏ Consistently Meets Expectations & Position Requirements
❏ Meets Some but not all Expectations & Position Requirements
❏ Does not meet Expectations & Position Requirements

Responsibility:
Specific Objectives:
Comments:

❑ Consistently & Significantly Exceeds Expectations & Position Requirements
❑ Consistently Meets & Sometimes Exceeds Expectations & Position Requirements
❑ Consistently Meets Expectations & Position Requirements
❑ Meets Some but not all Expectations & Position Requirements
❑ Does not meet Expectations & Position Requirements

Responsibility:
Specific Objectives:
Comments:

❑ Consistently & Significantly Exceeds Expectations & Position Requirements
❑ Consistently Meets & Sometimes Exceeds Expectations & Position Requirements
❑ Consistently Meets Expectations & Position Requirements
❑ Meets Some but not all Expectations & Position Requirements
❑ Does not meet Expectations & Position Requirements

Responsibility:
Specific Objectives:
Comments:

❑ Consistently & Significantly Exceeds Expectations & Position Requirements
❑ Consistently Meets & Sometimes Exceeds Expectations & Position Requirements
❑ Consistently Meets Expectations & Position Requirements
❑ Meets Some but not all Expectations & Position Requirements
❑ Does not meet Expectations & Position Requirements

Section 2: Core Behaviors

This section contains core behaviors that characterize the association's Statement of Philosophy and that the association expects of each associate. Rate the associate's performance in each area and, where appropriate and applicable, provide examples to support the rating.

Core Behavior: **Teamwork**
Specific Objectives: Willingly cooperates with others and places shared goals before narrower interests. Is receptive and responsive to others' ideas and opinions. Is personally effective as a team member.

Comments:

☐ Consistently & Significantly Exceeds Expectations & Position Requirements
☐ Consistently Meets & Sometimes Exceeds Expectations & Position Requirements
☐ Consistently Meets Expectations & Position Requirements
☐ Meets Some but not all Expectations & Position Requirements
☐ Does not meet Expectations & Position Requirements

Core Behavior: **Problem-Solving**
Specific Objectives: Identifies and defines problems, evaluates information and develops alternative solutions. Faces problems willingly and with a positive attitude. Follows up quickly and, whenever possible, personally.

Comments:

☐ Consistently & Significantly Exceeds Expectations & Position Requirements
☐ Consistently Meets & Sometimes Exceeds Expectations & Position Requirements
☐ Consistently Meets Expectations & Position Requirements
☐ Meets Some but not all Expectations & Position Requirements
☐ Does not meet Expectations & Position Requirements

Core Behavior:	**Initiative**
Objectives:	Suggests and/or initiates actions that will improve operations, use resources more creatively, and/or increase the efficiency and effectiveness of the work being done. Takes actions that are necessary and appropriate to meet organizational needs—not necessarily at the direction of the supervisor.
Comments:	

❑ Consistently & Significantly Exceeds Expectations & Position Requirements
❑ Consistently Meets & Sometimes Exceeds Expectations & Position Requirements
❑ Consistently Meets Expectations & Position Requirements
❑ Meets Some but not all Expectations & Position Requirements
❑ Does not meet Expectations & Position Requirements

Core Behavior:	**Personal Responsibility**
Objectives:	Takes ownership of the job. Willingly accepts authority and accountability for accomplishing results in carrying out the key job responsibilities.
Comments:	

❑ Consistently & Significantly Exceeds Expectations & Position Requirements
❑ Consistently Meets & Sometimes Exceeds Expectations & Position Requirements
❑ Consistently Meets Expectations & Position Requirements
❑ Meets Some but not all Expectations & Position Requirements
❑ Does not meet Expectations & Position Requirements

Core Behavior:	**Service Attitude**
Objectives:	Recognizes that we work for our membership and other internal and external constituents. Anticipates their needs and responds in a timely, positive manner. Embraces service challenges and finds ways to overcome obstacles to providing high quality support.
Comments:	

❑ Consistently & Significantly Exceeds Expectations & Position Requirements
❑ Consistently Meets & Sometimes Exceeds Expectations & Position Requirements
❑ Consistently Meets Expectations & Position Requirements
❑ Meets Some but not all Expectations & Position Requirements
❑ Does not meet Expectations & Position Requirements

Core Behavior:	**Professional Responsibility**
Objectives:	Focuses activities on accomplishing association objectives. Works within budgets. Makes no permanent enemies— remembers that "this is not personal." Treats others with respect.
Comments:	

❑ Consistently & Significantly Exceeds Expectations & Position Requirements
❑ Consistently Meets & Sometimes Exceeds Expectations & Position Requirements
❑ Consistently Meets Expectations & Position Requirements
❑ Meets Some but not all Expectations & Position Requirements
❑ Does not meet Expectations & Position Requirements

Section 3: Development Plan

List areas where development efforts will be concentrated during the coming year. Activities can be drawn from any of the following categories:

• On-the-job experience	(new assignments or special projects)
• In-house training	(association offered seminars and workshops)
• Outside training	(seminars, workshops, or courses offered outside the association)
• Professional development	(involvement in organizations, committees, and conferences)
• Other	(internal or external resources—videos, books, manuals)

Focus of Development Effort	Activities to Undertake	Time-Frame to Complete Activities

Section 4: Overall Rating

After rating each of the job responsibilities and core behaviors, develop an overall performance rating for the associate.

☐ Consistently & Significantly Exceeds Expectations & Position Requirements
☐ Consistently Meets & Sometimes Exceeds Expectations & Position Requirements
☐ Consistently Meets Expectations & Position Requirements
☐ Meets Some but not all Expectations & Position Requirements
☐ Does not meet Expectations & Position Requirements

Additional Supervisory Comments (include any changes/ additions to key job responsibilities):

Associate Comments:

Section 5: Year-End Signatures and Approvals

We have completed the Performance Plan and Review for the current review cycle, have met and discussed each area and agreed upon goals for the next review cycle.

_____
Supervisor's Signature   Date

_____
Associate's Signature   Date

I have reviewed this performance appraisal with my supervisor and have been given a copy for my records.

_____
Next Level Supervisor's Signature   Date

_____
Division Head's Signature   Date
Next Annual Review Date _____

PERFORMANCE PLAN & REVIEW
Progress Discussion Notes

Periodically throughout the performance plan year, supervisors should meet with associates to provide feedback, to commend performance that is above expectations, to note improvements that were made since the last review and/or to note where improvement is still needed. This will help to ensure that performance expectations are clearly communicated and understood throughout the plan year, that the associate has an opportunity to regularly discuss where he/she may need guidance or support from the supervisor, and to identify training needs or career aspirations. Any changes or additions to the associate's key job responsibilities since the last review should be discussed during these meetings and noted below.

Progress meetings should be held with the associate on a quarterly basis. Use the space below to make notes on issues discussed during these progress meetings. Both the supervisor and the associate should sign and date to indicate what items were discussed. These notes should be reviewed when completing the Annual Review Form.

Progress Discussion #1
Date of Meeting:_____
Issues Discussed:

Changes/Additions to Key Job Responsibilities:

_____
Supervisor's Signature   Date
_____
Associate's Signature   Date

Progress Discussion #2
Date of Meeting:_____
Issues Discussed:

Changes/Additions to Key Job Responsibilities:

_____
Supervisor's Signature   Date
_____
Associate's Signature   Date

Progress Discussion #3
Date of Meeting:_____
Issues Discussed:

Changes/Additions to Key Job Responsibilities:

_____
Supervisor's Signature   Date
_____
Associate's Signature   Date

Sample Performance Appraisal Form #7

Used by permission of Fried, Frank, Harris, Shriver & Jacobson LLP.

Each appraisal is individually prepared based on the appropriate job description.

PERFORMANCE EVALUATION
(For Non-Exempt and Professional Administrative Staff)

Employee:
Reviewer:
Position: HR/Benefits Jr. Analyst
Director:
Department: Human Resources
Last Review Date: _____
Division: Administration
Date of Review: _____
Part I: Primary Responsibilities

Rating Scale:

4 = *Exceeds Expectations* - Overall performance is exceptional. The employee demonstrates superior skills, creativity and personal effort in substantially exceeding performance standards.

3 = *Meets Expectations* - The employee is conscientious and consistently meets performance standards. Contributions made have been valuable to the Firm and department.

2 = *Partially Meets Expectations* - Overall performance meets some but not all of the position requirements. Performance in one or more areas of responsibility is either below expectations or not at a consistent and sustained level of achievement. The employee must improve performance in specified areas to bring results to a *Meets Expectations* level.

1 = *Does Not Meet Expectations* - Overall performance is below minimum standards and expectations. The employee has demonstrated a lack of required skills, knowledge, and/or effort. Performance at this level requires immediate, sustained improvement and may necessitate further disciplinary action.

N/A = Not Applicable

List the primary responsibilities from the position description. The appraiser should assign to each responsibility the rating which most accurately describes the employee's performance. Qualitative as well as quantitative/observable measures should be used in planning and evaluating performance. If the employee has more primary responsibilities than listed below, please add them in the space(s) provided and attach an additional sheet if necessary. Please provide comments in all categories.

PRIMARY BENEFITS

Responsibility: **Rating:** _____
Responsible for processing benefits enrollment and benefits termination for legal staff enrolled in the HTH overseas medical plans. Acts as intermediary between legal staff and HTH insurance carriers to resolve any problems, processes claims and premium payments.
Comments:

Responsibility: **Rating:** _____
Assists the Benefits Analysts in conducting benefits orientation for new staff, processing enrollment forms for medical/dental plans and COBRA information.
Comments:

Responsibility: **Rating:** _____
Assists the Benefits Analysts in processing claims for wage continuation and disability plans, including FMLA, NYSD and worker's compensation.
Comments:

Responsibility: **Rating:** _____
Assist with Health Club enrollment and administration.
Comments:

Responsibility: **Rating:** _____
Assist the Benefits Analysts in data entering of beneficiary information for Life and LTD benefit plans.
Comments:

Responsibility: **Rating:** _____
Assist with Partner and Employee Beneficiary Designation inquiries and changes.
Comments:

Responsibility: **Rating:** _____
Assist the Benefits Analysts with special benefits projects, such as Health Fair, CPR/AED Certification, Blood Drives, Weight/ Watchers, quarterly benefits auditing, as required.
Comments:

PRIMARY HUMAN RESOURCES

Responsibility: **Rating:** _____
Provides general administrative and clerical support to the Human Resources and Benefits Department.
Comments:

Responsibility: **Rating:** _____
Screens incoming calls and responds to general inquiries to include requests for employment verifications, reference requests, mortgage verifications, unemployment insurance, etc., greets and assists all guests at the front desk and sorts department mail.
Comments:

Responsibility: **Rating:** _____
Establishes and maintains relationships with managers to understand temporary staffing needs. Assists with filling temporary staff requests, maintaining temporary staffing agency relationships and agreements, requesting criminal/credit back ground checks, and maintaining updated status of temporary staff at the Firm.
Comments:

Responsibility: **Rating:** _____

Maintains current the administrative procedures manual, HR Intranet page, ie, discounts, employee handbook updates, etc.

Comments:

Responsibility: **Rating:** _____

Processes invoices for all HR Managers and maintains information on dollars spent in appropriate budget accounts. Assists with processing tuition reimbursement requests.

Comments:

Responsibility: **Rating:** _____

Assists with the employee recognition program, staff appreciation day functions, the annual milestone anniversary program, assists with employee in-house seminars, and coordinates Retirement parties.

Comments:

Responsibility: **Rating:** _____

Responsible for ordering and/or distribution of Firm anniversary gifts, employee gifts for births/weddings, ordering of flowers for death/illnesses.

Comments:

Responsibility: **Rating:** _____

Serves as back-up for the Benefits Analysts and Human Resources Assistant.

Comments:

Part II: Performance Factors

This section is comprised of factors which directly affect how well an employee does his/her job and should be considered in determining an overall rating of performance. Comments are encouraged on any factor, however, they are **required** on those evaluated as *Exceeds Expectations* (4), *Partially Meets Expectations* (2) and *Does Not Meet Expectations* (1).

_____

_____

Quantity/Quality of Work: Rating: _____

Overall, consistently produces an acceptable volume of work in relation to time, established standards, and conditions in the department. Consistently produces thorough, neat and accurate work.

Comments:

Dependability/Flexibility: Rating: _____

Consistently follows through on assignments and responsibilities; adapts well to change and supports change; flexible to working overtime when requested.

Comments:

Time Management: Rating: _____

Consistently produces an acceptable volume of work in relation to time, established standards, and conditions in the department. Organizes work well and uses time effectively. Meets established deadlines Works well under pressure.

Comments:

Interpersonal Relationships/Communication/Cooperation/ Teamwork: Rating: _____

Relates in a positive, professional and cooperative manner with co-workers, supervisors and other staff members toward common goal. Shares information in a timely manner; keeps appropriate people informed; listens, understands, uses confidential information with discretion; writes and speaks in a clear, concise manner. Supports the Firm and departmental plans, programs, policies, procedures and assists other team members.

Comments:

Initiative/Judgment: **Rating:** _____

Willingly assumes new and challenging assignments; is self-directed and motivated. Anticipates what needs to be done and does it. Offers creative, innovative and workable solutions. Exercises good judgment and knows when to consult.

Comments:

Acceptance of Criticism: **Rating:** _____

Accepts constructive criticism, learns from it and improves personal performance.

Comments:

Attendance and Punctuality: _____ **Sick** _____ **Lateness**
Rating: _____
Comments:

Part III: Significant Contributions and Accomplishments

Using the space below, focus on significant contributions and/or accomplishments the employee has made during the appraisal period.

Part IV: Professional Growth and Development (If applicable)

Based on the overall performance and the competencies required for success in the present position, list the developmental objectives that the employee and manager agree to achieve in the next 12 months. The primary focus should be on improving the employee's performance in their present job. Secondary emphasis should be placed on preparation for possible future assignments.

1. _____
2. _____
3. _____
4. _____
5. _____

Use the developmental action plan format below to indicate specific actions that will be taken to improve the employee's performance. Be sure to indicate who will initiate the action and when it will take place. Additional pages may be added if necessary.

Developmental Objective	How to Achieve	Target Date	How Competence Will be Measured

Part V: Appraisal Summary

Provide a summary rating of overall performance. This rating should reflect overall performance during the appraisal period and include performance against ongoing job responsibilities, previously agreed upon objectives and special projects. It should reflect both quantitative and qualitative assessments of performance.

_____ Exceeds Expectations
_____ Meets Expectations
_____ Partially Meets Expectations
_____ Does Not Meet Expectations

Employee Comments:

Part VI: Signatures

Note: Signature does not indicate agreement/disagreement

Employee's Signature: _____ Date: _____
Reviewer's Signature: _____ Date: _____
Director's Signature: _____ Date: _____

Sample Performance Appraisal Form #8

Used by permission of Columbia Lighthouse for the Blind

Employee: _____

Department: _____

Title: _____

Review Period: _____ to _____

INSTRUCTIONS

In completing this appraisal, the following sequence should be followed:

1. <u>Employee</u> completes page one (1), Performance Assessment, and reviews the job description provided by Human Resources. The completed Performance Assessment should be turned in to the supervisor. ***Complete by*** _____.

2. <u>Supervisor</u> completes pages two (2) through eleven (11) by indicating the appropriate numerical value. To determine the overall performance ranking (simple average) on page ten, add the numerical values together and divide by eight. **Note:** If the employee has supervisory responsibilities, complete the supervisory section as well. The divisor will then be twelve. Review the job description provided by Human Resources.
    Complete by _____.

3. <u>Supervisor</u> combines each employee's Performance Assessment with the rankings page and obtains the signature of their supervisor for each of their direct report's review form(s).
    Complete by _____.

4. <u>Supervisors</u> will, upon receipt of approval signatures, discuss the review and the current job description with the employee. ***Complete by*** _____.

5. **Employees** should sign and date the review form **and** the job description. Notify Human Resources of any changes/additions to the job description. ***Complete by*** _____.

6. Supervisors will return the signed Performance Review to Human Resources for permanent filing once they discuss the appraisal with the employee and obtain their signature. ***Complete by*** _____.

Employee: **PERFORMANCE ASSESSMENT**

Noteworthy (strong) areas of present performance:

_____

_____

Opportunities for improvement in job performance:

_____

_____

What performance areas have improved since the previous review?

_____

_____

Accomplishments since last review:

_____

_____

List no more than five (5) goals for the coming year:

_____

_____

Supervisors: Indicate the appropriate numerical value in the blank based on the following scale. Note that you must support Exceptional and Unsatisfactory rankings with specific examples for each.

5	**Exceptional** *
4	**Exceeds Expectations**
3	**Meets Expectations**
2	**Needs Improvement**
1	**Unsatisfactory** **

1. JOB KNOWLEDGE

Knowledge of products, policies and procedures; OR knowledge of techniques, skills, equipment, procedures, and materials.

___ Expert in job, has thorough grasp of all phases of job. (5)

___ Very well informed, seldom requires assistance and instruction. (4)

___ Satisfactory job knowledge, understands and performs most phases of job well, occasionally requires assistance or instruction. (3)

___ Limited knowledge of job, further training required, frequently requires assistance or instruction. (2)

___ Lacks knowledge to perform job properly. (1)

Comments, required for a rating of "Unsatisfactory" (1) or "Exceptional" (5): _____

2. QUALITY OF WORK

Freedom from errors and mistakes. Accuracy, quality of work in general.

___ Highest quality possible, final job virtually perfect. (5)

___ Quality above average with very few errors and mistakes. (4)

___ Quality very satisfactory, usually produces error free work. (3)

___ Room for improvement, frequent errors, work requires checking & re-doing. (2)

___ Excessive errors and mistakes, very poor quality. (1)

Comments, required for a rating of "Unsatisfactory" (1) or "Exceptional" (5): _____

3. COMMUNICATION

Uses proper oral and written language. Demonstrates good judgment in selecting proper means of communication. Listens actively and seeks clarification when needed. Keeps other departments informed of developments affecting their functions. Promptly responds to requests. Excels in dealing with the public – consumers, volunteers, donors.

___ Excels at communicating effectively both internally and externally. (5)

___ Above average communication skills; messages are always clear. (4)

___ Demonstrates effective communication on all levels. (3)

___ Needs improvement in communication with staff and/or public; messages are not clearly communicated. (2)

___ Lacking in effective communication skills; uses inappropriate means of communication. (1)

Comments, required for a rating of "Unsatisfactory" (1) or "Exceptional" (5): _____

4. QUANTITY OF WORK

Work output of the employee.

___ High volume producer, always does more than is expected or required. (5)

___ Produces more than most, above average. (4)

___ Handles a satisfactory volume of work, occasionally does more than is required. (3)

___ Barely acceptable, low output, below average. (2)

___ Extremely low output, not acceptable. (1)

Comments, required for a rating of "Unsatisfactory" (1) or "Exceptional" (5): _____

5. RELIABILITY

The extent to which the employee can be depended upon to be available for work, do it properly, and complete it on time. The degree to which the employee is reliable, trustworthy, and persistent.

___ Highly persistent, always gets the job done on time. (5)

___ Very reliable, above average, usually persists in spite ofdifficulties. (4)

___ Usually gets the job done on time, works well under pressure. (3)

___ Sometimes unreliable, will avoid responsibility, satisfied to dothe bare minimum. (2)

___ Usually unreliable, does not accept responsibility, gives up easily. (1)

Comments, required for a rating of "Unsatisfactory" (1) or "Exceptional" (5): _____

6. INITIATIVE AND CREATIVITY

The ability to plan work and to go ahead with a task without being told every detail, and the ability to make constructive suggestions.

___ Displays unusual drive and perseverance, anticipates neededactions, frequently suggests better ways of doing things. (5)

___ A self starter, proceeds on own with little or no direction, progressive, makes some suggestions for improvement. (4)

___ Very good performance, shows initiative in completing tasks. (3)

___ Does not proceed on own, waits for direction, routine worker. (2)

___ Lacks initiative, less than satisfactory performance. (1)

Comments, required for a rating of "Unsatisfactory" (1) or "Exceptional" (5): _____

7. JUDGEMENT

The extent to which the employee makes decisions which are sound. Ability to base decisions on fact rather than emotion.

___ Uses exceptionally good judgment when analyzing facts and solving problems. (5)

___ Above average judgment, thinking is very mature and sound. (4)

___ Handles most situations very well and makes sound decisions under normal circumstances. (3)

___ Uses questionable judgment at times, room for improvement. (2)

___ Uses poor judgment when dealing with people and situations. (1)

Comments, required for a rating of "Unsatisfactory" (1) or "Exceptional" (5): _____

8. COOPERATION

Willingness to work harmoniously with others in getting a job done. Readiness to respond positively to instructions and procedures.

___ Extremely cooperative, stimulates teamwork and good attitude in others. (5)

___ Goes out of the way to cooperate and get along. (4)

___ Cooperative, gets along well with others. (3)

___ Indifferent, makes little effort to cooperate or is disruptive to the overall group or department. (2)

___ Negative and hard to get along with. (1)

Comments, required for a rating of "Unsatisfactory" (1) or "Exceptional" (5): _____

COMPLETE THE FOLLOWING SECTION FOR SUPERVISORY PERSONNEL ONLY

9. (Supervisors Only) PLANNING, ORGANIZING, & PRIORITIZING

The ability to analyze work, set goals, develop plans of action, utilize time. Consider amount of supervision required and extent to which you can trust employee to carry out assignments conscientiously.

___ Exceptionally good planning and organizing skills. Conscientious. (5)

___ Above average planning and organizing. Usually carries out assignments conscientiously. (4)

___ Average planning and organizing. Occasionally requires assistance. (3)

___ Room for improvement. Frequently requires assistance. (2)

___ Unacceptable planning and organizing skills. (1)

Comments, required for a rating of "Unsatisfactory" (1) or "Exceptional" (5): _____

10. (Supervisors Only) COACHING & MENTORING

The ability to create a motivating climate, achieve teamwork, train and develop, measure work in progress, take corrective action.

___ Exceptional leader, others look up to this employee. (5)

___ Above average. Usually, but not always motivational. (4)

___ Average. Sometimes needs to be reminded of leadership role. (3)

___ Needs to improve motivational and teamwork skills. (2)

___ Unacceptable directing and controlling skills. (1)

Comments, required for a rating of "Unsatisfactory" (1) or "Exceptional" (5): _____

11. (Supervisors Only) DECISION-MAKING

The ability to make decisions and the quality and timeliness of those decisions.

___ Exceptional decision making abilities. Decisions are made in a timely manner. (5)

___ Above average decision making abilities. Usually makes sound and timely decisions. (4)

___ Average. Sometimes requires assistance in making decisions. (3)

___ Needs to improve decision making and/or timeliness of decisions. (2)

___ Unacceptable decisions and/or timeliness. (1)

Comments, required for a rating of "Unsatisfactory" (1) or "Exceptional" (5): _____

12. (Supervisors Only) INTERPERSONAL SKILLS/ NEGOTIATION & CONFLICT MANAGEMENT

Builds trust and rapport among staff while recognizing the opinions and needs of others. Conveys a positive personal image and develops positive working relationships. Successfully prevents conflicts from arising and excels at resolving conflicts when they do arise by identifying issues and concerns of all parties.

____ Exceptional ability to deflect conflict and resolve issues before they become a conflict. Demonstrates appreciation for the opinion of others. (5)

____ Above average negotiating abilities. Usually prevents conflicts through negotiation. (4)

____ Average. Occasionally requires assistance in resolving conflicts. (3)

____ Needs to improve negotiation skills. (2)

____ Ineffective management of conflicts and negotiations. (1)

Comments, required for a rating of "Unsatisfactory" (1) or "Exceptional" (5): _____

PERFORMANCE LEVELS

EXCEPTIONAL (5)
Truly outstanding performance that results in extraordinary and exceptional accomplishments with significant contributions to objectives of the department, division, group or company.

EXCEEDS EXPECTATIONS (4)
Consistently generates results above those expected of the position. Contributes in a superior manner to innovations both technical and functional.

MEETS EXPECTATIONS (3)
Good performance with incumbent fulfilling all position requirements and may on occasion generate results above those expected of the position.

NEEDS IMPROVEMENT (2)
Performance leaves room for improvement. This performance level may be the result of new or inexperienced incumbent on the job or an incumbent not responding favorably to instruction.

UNSATISFACTORY (1)
Lowest performance level which is clearly less than acceptable, and which is obviously well below minimum position requirements. Situation requires immediate review and action. Possible separation or reassignment is in order without significant and immediate performance improvement.

Overall Performance Rating:
Cumulative: _____
Divided by 8 (or 12): _____

Select one category below:
5   **Exceptional** *
4   **Exceeds Expectations**
3   **Meets Expectations**
2   **Needs Improvement**
1   **Unsastifactory** **

* Written justification for 'distinguished' performance must be submitted to the department head and human resources prior to discussion with the employee.

**A detailed plan to address "unsatisfactory" performers must be submitted to the department head and human resources, prior to the performance discussion with the employee.

EMPLOYEE COMMENTS:

_____
_____
_____

SIGNATURES: Signatures acknowledge that this form was discussed and reviewed.

Employee: _____ Date: _____

Prepared by: _____ Date: _____
              Supervisor

Approved by: _____ Date: _____
              Supervisor's Supervisor

Sample Performance Appraisal Form #9

Used by permission of the Farmington Country Club.

PERFORMANCE REVIEW

Employee: _____ Reviewer: _____
Position/Job Title: _____ Position/Job Title: _____
Date of Review: _____ Period Covered by Review: _____

This review is a tool for improving performance. When done properly, it will highlight strengths and accomplishments while identifying areas for improvement in the future. In completing this review, please take the time to carefully and fairly consider the performance of the person being reviewed for the entire period covered by the review.

To ensure a consistent perspective and vocabulary for all reviews, we describe performance suing the following six terms:

LETTER
CODE

GE **Greatly Exceeds Expectation**: Significantly and consistently exceeds standards and expectations

E **Exceeds Expectation:** Exceeds standards and expectations

M **Meets Expectation:** Meets standards and expectations

BID **Below Expectation, Improvement Desired:** Does not meet standards and expectations

BIE **Below Expectation, Improvement Essential:** Significantly below standards and expectations

NA **Not Applicable:** This aspect of performance is not relevant to position

On the page that follows, various components of job performance are listed. In the space to the left of each statement, please indicate your review of this employee's performance by using the letter codes from the definitions provided above.

In the Comments section, provide specific examples of the employee's job performance that illustrate your review, and identify the goals that were achieved and those that still need to be achieved.

The performance review form includes a separate page for you and the employee to identify individual knowledge and skill development goals and performance goals for the employee to achieve during the next review period. These goals should be measurable, realistic, and set within a specific timeframe for completion.

- During this performance review, complete columns 1-3 (Goal, Action Plan, Timetable for Completion
- During the next performance review, complete column 4 (Goal Achievement)

____	**Technical Knowledge**	Displays understanding of facts and concepts necessary to perform capably over time
____	**Applied Knowledge**	Is able to apply technical knowledge to job situations in ways that enhance performance
____	**Productivity**	Completes work with a high level of quality in the time allotted
____	**Work Quality**	Output meets the high standards of the Club
____	**Member Interaction**	Says "hello," makes eye contact and is helpful and courteous
____	**Leadership**	Sets high standards, communicates them in words and conduct, and serves as a teacher and a role model for co-workers
____	**Teamwork**	Gets along with other employees and willing pitches in when needed
____	**Communication**	Uses appropriate language and effectively conveys meaning
____	**Decision Making**	Carefully gathers all necessary information and considers alternatives before choosing one
____	**Independence**	Works with little or no supervision
____	**Initiative**	Seeks new tasks and opportunities to expand knowledge and ability

____	**Creativity**	Suggests ideas, discovers new and better ways of accomplishing individual and group goals
____	**Professionalism**	Maintains mature and dignified demeanor
____	**Attendance**	Is consistently on time and minimizes absences
____	**Dependability**	Can be relied on to complete responsibilities with a minimum of supervision and follow-up
____	**Adherence to Policy**	Is familiar and complies with relevant Club policies

Comments

Provide specific examples of the employee's job performance that illustrate your review, and identify the goals that were achieved and those that still need to be achieved. Your examples may describe:

- job performance that exceeded or greatly exceeded your expectations, improved during the review period, or needs improvement during the next review period; and
- goals that were achieved during the review period, or goals that were not achieved during the review period.

(Type Comments Here)

Signatures below indicate that a meeting took place to review the performance during the past review period and to establish knowledge and skill development goals and performance goals for the next review period.

_____

Employee Signature and Date

_____

Reviewer Signature and Date

_____

Department Head Signature and Date

_____

General Manager Signature and Date

_____

HR Manager Signature and Date

Employee: _____ Reviewer: _____
Position/Job Title: _____ Position/Job Title: _____
Period Covered by Goals: _____

Individual Knowledge and Skill Development Goals

Goal	Action plan	Timetable for completion	Goal achievement (Complete with next performance review)

Individual Performance Goals

Goal	Action plan	Timetable for completion	Goal achievement (Complete with next performance review)

Signatures below indicate that a meeting took place to review the performance during the past review period and to establish knowledge and skill development goals and performance goals for the next review period.

_____
Employee Signature and Date

_____
Reviewer Signature and Date

_____
Department Head Signature and Date

_____
General Manager Signature and Date

_____
HR Manager Signature and Date

Sample Performance Appraisal Form #10

Used by permission of the Farmington Country Club.

PERFORMANCE REVIEW

FOR MANAGERS AND SUPERVISORS

Employee: _____ Reviewer: _____
Position/Job Title: _____ Position/Job Title: _____
Date of Review: _____ Period Covered by Review: _____

This review is a tool for improving performance. When done properly, it will highlight strengths and accomplishments while identifying areas for improvement in the future. In completing this review, please take the time to carefully and fairly consider the performance of the person being reviewed for the entire period covered by the review.

To ensure a consistent perspective and vocabulary for all reviews, we describe performance suing the following six terms:

LETTER
CODE

GE Greatly Exceeds Expectation: Significantly and consistently exceeds standards and expectations

E Exceeds Expectation: Exceeds standards and expectations

M Meets Expectation: Meets standards and expectations

BID Below Expectation, Improvement Desired: Does not meet standards and expectations

BIE Below Expectation, Improvement Essential: Significantly below standards and expectations

NA Not Applicable: This aspect of performance is not relevant to position

On the page that follows, various components of job performance are listed. In the space to the left of each statement, please indicate your review of this employee's performance by using the letter codes from the definitions provided above.

In the Comments section, provide specific examples of the employee's job performance that illustrate your review, and identify the goals that were achieved and those that still need to be achieved.

The performance review form includes a separate page for you and the employee to identify individual knowledge and skill development goals and performance goals for the employee to achieve during the next review period. These goals should be measurable, realistic, and set within a specific timeframe for completion.

- During this performance review, complete columns 1-3 (Goal, Action Plan, Timetable for Completion
- During the next performance review, complete column 4 (Goal Achievement)

1. Management and Supervision

____ **Staff recruitment and hiring**

Takes an active and effective role in attracting new staff. Demonstrates an ability to select employees well-suited to their position.

____ **Feedback**

Provides regular feedback, both verbal and written, to improve employee performance—performance reviews are thorough and used a s a tool to guide development.

____ **Recognition**

Provides recognition, both tangible and intangible, to reinforce good performance.

____ **Directing and dealing with people**

Is confident, but keeps own ego in check. Displays concern for self-esteem of subordinates and treats all staff with respect and courtesy.

____ **Balance**

Dealings with staff reflect consistency, impartiality and sensitivity to their needs whenever possible. Keeps cool under pressure and maintains composure and objectivity when things do not happen as expected.

____ **Delegation**

Is comfortable delegating both responsibility and authority. Understands which tasks are best given to subordinates to enhance team efficiency.

____ **Development of subordinates**

Is committed to and enjoys training. Seeks opportunities for subordinates to grow and learn. Willing to take prudent risks to develop the skills of staff. Tests and challenges the abilities of subordinates with developmental outcome in mind.

____ **Creating and maintaining standards**

Communicates clear and tangible standards for performance. Consistently enforces work standards and rules and does not make exceptions based on personal likes and dislikes.

____ **Focuses on and achieves results**
Demonstrates commitment to attaining goals in spite of problems or obstacles that may arise. Makes decisions and takes action based on the intended result rather than the needs of the process. Does not confuse effort with successful outcome.

2. Communication

____ **Speaking skills**
Speaks well, conveying information and ideas effectively. Changes vocabulary and style of speech to suit situation and the background of the audience to whom he or she is speaking.

____ **Listening skills**
Is a good active listener. When listening to others, asks questions to indicate interest, gain specific information and to confirm understanding. Admits when he/she does not understand or is confused and asks for clarification.

____ **Writing skills**
Writes clearly and concisely, organizes thoughts well and attends to the rules of grammar, syntax, punctuation, etc.

____ **Meeting skills**
Is prepared for and actively participates in meetings. Is an effective meeting leader. Uses meetings when appropriate and displays understanding of how to organize an effective meeting.

____ **Communicates effectively**
Provides the right information to the right people at the right time. Informs supervisor of issues, activities, and plans on a regular basis.

3. Leadership

____ **Models the way**
Is clear about personal philosophy of leadership. Sets an example of what is expected. Communicates and builds consensus around the Club's mission, vision, and core values, and behaves in a manner consistent with them. Personally accepts responsibility for performance in his or her area of responsibility. Ensures that people adhere to agreed-upon standards. Follows through on promises and commitments.

____ **Inspires a shared vision**
Appeals to others to share a dream of the future and shows them how their interests can be realized. Finds ways to align personal values and operating goals with the larger Club vision. Knows constituents and is able to relate to them in ways that energize and uplift them. Motivates others to follow by building consensus. Speaks with conviction about the meaning of work.

_____ **Challenges the process**
Reforms "from the inside." Continually strives to achieve goals, improve on past performance, and exceed expectations, no matter what the challenge. Embraces change; searches for opportunities to innovate, grow, and improve. Experiments, takes risks, and learns from mistakes. Challenges others to try new approaches. Searches outside the Club for innovative ways to improve.

____ **Enables others to act**
Develops relationships based on collaboration, trust, and mutual respect. Treats people with respect and dignity. Trusts others to use their discretion and authority. Encourages others to take risks, create change, and achieve results. Supports decisions others make and helps them learn from their mistakes. Actively listens to and considers diverse points of view. Involves "informal leaders" where possible.

____ **Encourages the heart**
Expresses confidence in people's abilities. Finds creative, genuine, and visible ways to recognize other people's contributions and celebrate accomplishments. Praises people a job well done. Promotes team spirit and maintains a positive outlook.

4. Organization and Planning

____ **Organizes time and uses efficiently**
Uses daily "to do list," day timer and calendar to organize time and work efficiently.

____ **Maintains orderly workplace**
Maintains organized office space, including files, etc.—insists that staff maintain organized work flow to maximize efficiency.

____ **Uses "systems approach"**
Establishes and communicates a routine approach to frequent, redundant or predictable tasks—uses forms and checklists to ensure consistency.

____ **Anticipation and foresight**
Anticipates problems and unusual circumstances, and makes contingency plans. Anticipates implications of actions two and three steps beyond immediate situation. Evaluates decisions in terms of their effect on the immediate and long term and is aware of precedent as it is being set.

____ **Priority orientation**
Manages time wisely and focuses efforts on areas that are most important or of most lasting significance. Demonstrates understanding of how various activities and projects fit into the "big picture."

5. Professional and Technical Competence

____   **Technical knowledge**
Demonstrates the technical knowledge necessary to perform effectively. Is current on emerging technical, professional and industrial developments.

____   **Applied knowledge**
Consistently utilizes technical knowledge to enhance performance. Seeks opportunities to utilize newly-acquired or newly-developed expertise.

6. Teamwork

____   **Sensitive to the morale of the team**
Accepts responsibility for the morale of the team—works to build alliances and to resolve conflict within the group.

____   **Develops "team solutions"**
Obtains agreement and acceptance by soliciting and utilizing the ideas of others. Actively involves staff at all levels of the organization and includes "informal leaders" where possible.

____   **Provides support to the team**
Works to support the decisions of peers and superiors even if he/she disagrees with them. Meets with other members of the team to coordinate efforts and solve problems through mutual dialogue.

____   **Respects "the system"**
Understands the organization, distribution of authority and chain of command—uses appropriate channels to communicate and achieve outcomes.

7. Entrepreneurship

____   **Can translate decisions into dollars**
Understands the financial implications of decision making and can anticipate the impact of actions and products.

____   **Opportunistic**
Develops and implements strategies to exploit opportunities and to further the financial goals of the organization. Reacts quickly to changes and challenges which arise.

____   **"Sells" the club**
Develops contacts, enhances the Club's image and promotes its interests through visible participation in business, civic and professional organizations.

____   **Decision making and analysis**
Carefully monitors important financial information to compare actual to budgeted financial performance. Makes decisions and takes action to ensure budgets are attained or exceeded.

8. **Customer Service**

This section deals with service to all customers, which in some instances refers to members and guests, and in others refers to staff members or other "internal customers." Although some staff members do not interact directly with members, etc., of equal importance is their interaction with co-works, vendors, etc. "If you're not serving the customer, you are serving someone who is."

____ **Anticipation**

Anticipates customer needs and takes action to deliver customer satisfaction within the limits of his/her authority.

____ **Responsive**

Reacts quickly and enthusiastically to customer requests.

____ **Builds relationships**

Maintains relationships in a manner which ensures the long term, "big picture" success of the whole organizations.

____ **Gets results**

Deals with complaints and problems personally, decisively and in a manner which assures that the customer leaves happy.

____ **"Champions the customer"**

Gives priority to customer preferences and emphasizes the legitimacy of customer expectations.

9. **Personal Development**

____ **Develops career plan**

Takes responsibility for fostering own personal and professional development.

____ **Sets goals**

Sets realistic professional goals and works to attain them.

____ **Builds contacts**

Makes industry contacts and circulates within a group of peer professionals.

____ **Community involvement**

Identifies opportunities to further Club's role in community, civic and charitable organizations.

Comments

Provide specific examples of the employee's job performance that illustrate your review, and identify the goals that were achieved and those that still need to be achieved. Your examples may describe:

- job performance that exceeded or greatly exceeded your expectations, improved during the review period, or needs improvement during the next review period; and
- goals that were achieved during the review period, or goals that were not achieved during the review period.

(Type Comments Here)

Signatures below indicate that a meeting took place to review the performance during the past review period and to establish knowledge and skill development goals and performance goals for the next review period.

Employee Signature and Date

Reviewer Signature and Date

Department Head Signature and Date

General Manager Signature and Date

HR Manager Signature and Date

Employee: _____ Reviewer: _____
Position/Job Title: _____ Position/Job Title: _____
Date of Review: _____ Period Covered by Review: _____

Individual Knowledge and Skill Development Goals

Goal	Action plan	Timetable for completion	Goal achievement (Complete with next performance review)

Individual Performance Goals

Goal	Action plan	Timetable for completion	Goal achievement (Complete with next performance review)

Signatures below indicate that a meeting took place to review the performance during the past review period and to establish knowledge and skill development goals and performance goals for the next review period.

Employee Signature and Date

Reviewer Signature and Date

Department Head Signature and Date

General Manager Signature and Date

HR Manager Signature and Date

Notes

Introduction

1. David Butcher, "It Takes Two to Review," *Management Today*, (London: Haymarket Publishing LTD, 2002), 54-59.

Chapter 1

1. Peter F. Drucker, *The Practice of Management*, (New York: Harper Business, 1986), 312.

2. Kenneth A. Kovach, *Strategic Human Resources Management*, (Maryland: University Press of America, 1996), 1-4.

3. Kovach, 4.

4. Wayne F. Cascio, *Managing Human Resources*, 6th ed., (New York: McGraw-Hill Higher Education, 2003), 330.

5. Susan Heathfield, "Performance Appraisals Don't Work," *Human Resources* [home page on-line]; available from *http://www.humanresources.guide@about.com*; accessed June 2000.

6. Angelo S. DeNisi and Ricky W. Griffin, *Human Resource Management*, (Massachusetts: Houghton Mifflin Company, 2001), 309.

Chapter 2

1. Henry Mintzberg, *The Manager's Job*, (Massachusetts: Harvard Business School Press, 1998), 23.

2. Matthew McKay, Martha Davis, and Patrick Fleming, *Messages*, (California: New Harbinger Publications, Inc., 1995), 167.

3. Ibid., 45.

4. Ibid., 47.

5. Karen McKirchey, *Powerful Performance Appraisals*, (New Jersey: Career Press, 1998), 21.

6. Marcus Buckingham and Curt Coffman, *First, Break All The Rules: What the World's Greatest Managers Do Differently*, (New York: Simon and Schuster, 1999), 226.

7. Drucker, 307.

8. H. Jackson Brown, Jr., ed., *A Father's Book of Wisdom*, (Tennessee: Rutledge Hill Press, 1988), 157.

9. Kovach, 13.

Chapter 3

1. Dennis M. Daley, *Strategic Human Resource Management–People and Performance Management in the Public Sector*, (Upper Saddle River, NJ: Prentice Hall, 2002), 186.

2. Ivancevich, 251, citing Mary N. Vinson (April 1996), "The Pros and Cons of 360-Degree Feedback: Making It Work," *Training and Development*, 11–12.

3. J. Samuel Bois, *The Art of Awareness*, 3rd ed., (Iowa: Wm. C. Brown Publishers, 1979), 240.

4. Edwin Newman, *Strictly Speaking*, (New York: The Bobbs-Merrill Company, 1974), 151.

5. Daley, 56.

6. Daley, 57.

7. Wayne R. Mondy et al, *Human Resource Management* (8th ed.), (New Jersey: Prentice Hall, 2002), 110.

8. Norman R. Augustine, *Reshaping an Industry*, (Massachusetts: Harvard Business School Press, 1998), 182–83.

9. John C. Maxwell, *The 17 Essential Qualities of A Team Player*, (Tennessee: Thomas Nelson Publishers, 2002), 138.

10. Oren Harari, *The Leadership Secrets of Colin Powell*, (New York: McGraw-Hill, 2002), 33.

11. George R. Dreher and Thomas W. Dougherty, *Human Resource Strategy: A Behavioral Perspective for the General Manager*, (New York: McGraw-Hill/Irwin, 2002), 158.

12. McKay et al, 24–25.

13. Ibid., 35.

14. T. Redman et al., "Performance Appraisal in an NHS Hospital," *Human Resource Management Journal* 10. No. 1 (2002): 48–62.

15. Tony Moglia, *Partners in Performance, Successful Performance Management*, (California: Crisp Publications, Inc., 1997), 21.

Chapter 4

1. John P. Kotter, "Winning at Change," *Leader to Leader*, 10 (Fall 1998): 27-33.

2. Paul Lukas, "UPS: The Whole Package," *Fortune Small Business*, March 19, 2003.

3. Louis V. Gerstner, *Who Says Elephants Can't Dance*, (New York: Harper Business, 2002), dedication page.

4. Charles M. Farkas and Suzy Wetlaufer, *The Way Chief Executive Officers Lead*, (Boston: Harvard Business Review on Leadership, Harvard Business School Press, 1998), 28.

5. Discussion moderated by Harris Collingwood and Julia Kirby, *All in a Day's Work*, (Boston: Harvard Business Review on Breakthrough Leadership, Harvard Business School Press, 2001), 63.

6. James C. Collins and Jerry I. Porras, *Building Your Company's Vision*, (Boston: Harvard Business Review on Change, Harvard Business School Press, 1998), 30.

7. Ibid., 26.

8. Drucker, 146.

9. Mary Hayes, "Goal Oriented," *Information Week*, 930, (March 10, 2003): 35.

10. Ibid., 36.

11. Omar Aguilar, "How Strategic Performance Management is Helping Companies Create Business Value," *Strategic Finance*, 87, no. 7, (January 2003): 48.

12. Ibid., 49.

13. Drucker, 64.

14. Ibid., 124.

15. J. Samuel Bois, *The Art of Awareness*, (Dubuque, Iowa: Wm. C. Brown Publishers, 1978), 289.

16. Maxwell, 95.

17. Stephen J. Brewer, "Aligning Human Capital in Achieving Business Goals and Strategic Objectives," SHRM White Paper, September, 2000, Reviewed March 2002.

18. Collingwood and Kirby, 58.

19. Raymond Noe, John Hollenbeck, Barry Gerhart, Patrick Wright, *Human Resource Management: Gaining a Competitive Advantage*, 3rd ed., (New York: McGraw-Hill/Irwin, 2000), 292.

20. Ivancevich, 261.

Chapter 5

1. Donald L. Caruth and Gail D. Handlogten, *Managing Compensation (and Understanding It Too)*, (Connecticut: Quorum Books, 2001), 1.

2. Ibid., 2, as quoted from Donald L. Caruth, *Compensation Management for Banks* (Boston: Bankers Publishing, 1986), 7.

3. Ibid., 1.

4. Robert L. Mathis and John H Jackson, *Human Resources Management*, 10th ed., (Mason, OH: South-Western College Publications, 2003), 375.

5. Ibid.

6. Jeffrey Pfeffer, *Six Dangerous Myths About Pay*, (Boston: Harvard Business Review on Managing People, Harvard Business School Press, 1999), 94.

7. Terry Satterfield, "Speaking of Pay," *HR Magazine*, 48, no. 3, (March 2003): 99–101.

8. Ibid.

9. Caruth as cite 11, 170, as quoted from *Compensation*, 6th ed., George T. Milkovich and Jerry M. Newman, (Boston: McGraw-Hill/Irwin, 1999), 410–412.

10. Satterfield, 99–101.

11. Caruth, 45.

12. Satterfield, 99–101.

13. Ivancevich, 335–336.

14. Lance A. Berger and Dorothy R. Berger, eds., *The Compensation Handbook*, 4th ed., (New York: McGraw-Hill, 1999), 132–133.

15. Mathis, 373.

16. James W. Smither, ed., *Performance Appraisal: State of the Art in Practice*, (San Francisco, CA: John Wiley & Sons, Inc., 1998), 506.

17. Berger, 200.

18. H. H. Altmansberger and M. Wallace, "Designing a Goal-Sharing Program." *American Compensation Association (ACA) Building Blocks*, Scottsdale, AZ, 1998.

19. Ivancevich, 311.

20. Scott Hays, "Pros and Cons of Pay for Performance", *ZPG* [home page on-line]; available from *http://www.zigonperf.com/resources/pmnews/proscons.html*; accessed 14 April 2003, quoting Alfie Kohn.

21. Ibid.

22. Hays.

23. Pfeffer, 89-90.

24. Ibid.

25. Nelson, 104.

26. Ibid.

Chapter 6

1. Shimon L. Dolan and Denis Moran, "The Effects of Rater-Ratee Relationship on Ratee Perceptions of the Appraisal Process," *Human Resource Management*, 8th ed., (New York: McGraw-Hill/Irwin, 2001), 337–351.

2. Drucker, 81–82.

3. DeNisi and Griffin, 250.

4. DeNisi, 7.

5. Sanford M. Jacoby, A Century of Human Resource Management, from a paper presented at the 75th Anniversary Conference of Industrial Relations Counselors, Princeton University, September 11, 2001.

6. David Day et al., *HR Briefing*, (New York: Aspen Publishers, July 1, 2002), 7.

7. Jane Halpert, Midge Wilson, Julia Hickman, "Pregnancy as a Source of Bias in Performance Appraisals," *Journal of Organizational Behavior* 14 (1993): 655.

8. William S. Swan, *How To Do a Superior Performance Appraisal*, (New York: John Wiley & Sons, 1991), 120.

9. Ibid., 121.

10. H. John Bernardin and Richard W. Beatty, *Performance Appraisal: Assessing Human Behavior at Work*, (Boston: Kent Publishing, 1984), 140.

11. E.D. Pulakos, "The Development of Training Programs to Increase Accuracy on Different Rating Forms," *Organizational Behavior and Human Decision Processes*, 38 (1986): 76–91.

12. Jerry W. Hedge and Michael J. Kavanagh, "Improving the Accuracy of Performance Evaluations: Comparisons of Three Methods of Performance Appraiser Training," *Journal of Applied Psychology*, 68-73, in *Human Resource Management* (8th ed.), John M. Ivancevich, (New York: McGraw-Hill/Irwin, 2001), 268.

Chapter 7

1. Maxwell, 77–78.

2. Brian L. Davis et al., *The Successful Manager's Handbook: Development Suggestions for Today's Managers*, (Minneapolis, Minn.: Personnel Decisions International, 1992), 407.

3. Ferdinand Fournies, *Coaching*, (New York: McGraw-Hill, 2000), 68.

4. Ibid., 177.

5. Davis et al., 288.

6. Dr. Deborah Tannen, *That's Not What I Meant*, (New York: Ballantine Books, 1986), 61.

Chapter 8

1. *Carlton v. Mystic Transportation, Inc.* 202 F .3d 129 (2d Cir.).

2. *Burlington Indus., Inc. v. Ellerth*, 524 U.S. 742 (1998).

3. *Russell v. Principi*, 257 F. 3d 815 (D.C. Cir. 2001).

4. *McDonnell Douglas Corporation v. Green*, 411 U.S. 792 (1973).

5. *Texas Department of Community Affairs v. Burdine*, 450 U.S. 248 (1981).

6. *Brennan v. GTE Government Systems Corp.*, 150 F.3d 21 (1st Cir.).

7. *Rodriquez-Cuervos v. Wal-Mart Stores, Inc.*, 181 F3d 15 (1st Cir.).

8. C.F.R. 1201.56(c)(2). *U. S. Postal Service Board of Governors v. Aikens*, 460 U.S. 711 (1983); *Furnco Construction Company v. Waters*, 438 U.S. 567 (1978); *International Brotherhood of Teamsters v. United States*, 431 U.S. 324 (1977).

9. Protected activities are defined as: making a formal or informal complaint of discrimination; opposing a discriminatory work practice; and participating in either a discrimination investigation or court case.

10. *McKenna v. Weinberger*, 729 F.2d 783, 790 (D.C. Cir. 1984).

Chapter 9

1. Alvin Toffler, *Powershift*, (New York: Bantam Books, Bantam Doubleday Dell Publishing Group, 1990), 82.

2. Ibid., 82.

3. Table 5, Bureau of Labor Statistics, U.S. Department of Labor, Civilian Labor Force by Sex, Age, Race & Hispanic Origin 1990, 2000 and projected 2010 Civilian Population Survey.

4. Joanne Sujansky, "The Critical Care and Feeding of Generation Y," *Workforce*, 81, issue 5, (May 2002): 15.

5. Ibid.

6. Susan Parks, "Improving Workplace Performance: Historical and Theoretical Contexts," *Monthly Labor Review*, May 1995, 20, quoting Sanford Jacoby, *Employing Bureaucracy: Masters to Managers: Historical and Comparative Perspectives on American Employers*, (New York: Columbia University Press, 1991), 15.

7. "Keep Your Staff—Even Without the Big Pay Increases," *Accounting Office Management & Administration Report*, available from http://*www.smartbiz.com/article/view/176* [home page on-line]; accessed May 2003.

8. Alex Hiam, *Making Horses Drink*, (Irvine, CA: Entrepreneur Media, Inc., 2002), 76.

9. Ibid., 84.

10. Davis et al, 429.

11. Robert H. Schaffer and Harvey A. Thomson "Successful Change Programs Begin with Results" *Harvard Business Review on Change*, 70, issue 1 (January/February 1992): 80.

12. Maxwell, 80.

13. Ibid., 77.

14. Editors of Wall Street Journal, *Boss Talk—Top CEOs Share The Ideas That Drive the World's Most Successful Companies*, (Random House, NY, 2002), x.

15. Hiam, 31.

16. Beth Axelrod, Helen Handfield-Jones, and Ed Michaels "A New Game Plan for C Players," *Harvard Business Review*, (January 2002): 88.

17. Dayton Fandray, "The New Thinking in Performance Appraisals," *Workforce* 80, issue 5, (May 2001): 36.

18. Collins and Porras, 28–29.

19. Ibid.

20. T J Larkin and Sandar Larkin, *Communicating Change— Winning Employee Support for New Business Goals*, (New York: McGraw-Hill, Inc, 1994), xii.

21. Peter M. Senge, *The Fifth Discipline*, (New York: Currency/ Doubleday, 1994), 139.

22. Caruth and Handlogten, 220.

23. Aubrey C. Daniels, *Bringing Out the Best in People: How To Apply the Astonishing Power of Positive Reinforcement*, (New York: McGraw-Hill, Inc., 2000), 5.

24. Ron and Susan Zemke, "30 Things We Know For Sure About Adult Learning," *Training/HRD Magazine* (June 1981), and the work of John M. Carroll.

25. Robert H. Woods, *Managing Hospitality Human Resources*, 3rd ed., (Lansing, MI: Educational Institute of the American Hotel and Lodging Association, 2002), 232.

26. Fournies, 101.

27. Ibid., 102.

28. Drucker, 372.

29. Collins and Porras, 35.

30. Ibid.

31. Data based on the current population survey from the Bureau of Labor Statistics of the U.S. Department of Labor, press release, April 19, 2002.

32. Fay Hansen, "Introduction: Experts Debate the Future of the FLSA and the NLRA," *Compensation & Benefits Review* 28, no. 6 (July/August 1996) as cited in Mondy et al, 375.

33. David A. DeCenzo, Stephen P. Robbins, *Human Resource Management*, 6th ed., (Hoboken, NJ: Wiley and Sons, Inc., 1999), 115.

34. Department of Labor, Office of the Secretary. Telework and the New Workplace of the 21st Century Executive Summary. Retrieved June 1, 2003, from *www.dol.gov/asp/telework/execsum.htm*.

35. ITAC Website and Christina Heilig, "Workshop 10—Monitoring the Program, Planning the Expansion," ITAC, 1999.

36. Emma Keelan, "Two for One," *Accountancy*, (May, 2001): 40.

37. N. Cornelius, *Human Resource Management: A Managerial Perspective*, 2nd ed., (United Kingdom: Thompson Learning), citing Carol Norman and Robert Zwacki, "Team Appraisals-Team Approach," *Personnel Journal* 70, issue 9 (September 1991): 101.

38. Brickley, 148.

39. Carla Joinson, "Managing Virtual Teams," *HRMagazine* 47, no. 6, (June 2002): 68.

40. David Antonioni, "The Effects of Feedback Accountability on Upward Appraisal Ratings," *Personnel Psychology* 47, no. 2 (Summer, 1994): 349.

41. J. H. Bernardin and R. W. Beatty, "Can Subordinates Appraisals Enhance Managerial Productivity?," *Sloan Management Review* 28, issue 4, (Summer, 1987): 70–71.

42. Ivancevich, 384, adapted from Ron Zemke, Claire Raines and Bob Filipczak, "Generation Gaps in the Classroom," *Training* 36, issue 11, (November 1999): 48–54.

43. Louisa Wah, "Managing Gen Xers Strategically," *Management Review* 89, issue 3, (March 2000): 6.

44. Diane Thielfoldt and Devon Scheef, "Generation X and The Millennials: What You Need to Know About Mentoring the New Generations," *Law Practice TODAY*, November, 2004, an online publication of the American Bar Association's Law Practice Management section. Referenced September 1, 2009 at *www.abanet.org/lpm/lpt/articles/mgt0888044.html*.

45. Sujansky, 15.

46. Ibid.

47. Shannon L. Hatfield, "Understanding the Four Generations to Enhance Workplace Management," *AFP Exchange* 22, issue 4, (July/August 2002): 72.

Bibliography

Aguilar, Omar. "How Strategic Performance Management is Helping Companies Create Business Value." *Strategic Finance*, (January 2003): 48.

Altmansberger, H. H., and M. Wallace. "Designing a GoalSharing Program." *American Compensation Association (ACA) Building Blocks*, Scottsdale, AZ, 1998.

Antonioni, David. "The Effects of Feedback Accountability on Upward Appraisal Ratings." *Personnel Psychology* 47 (Summer 1994): 349.

Augustine, Norman R. *Reshaping an Industry*. Massachusetts: Harvard Business School Press, 1998.

Axelrod, Beth, et al. "A New Game Plan for C Players." *Harvard Business Review*, (January 2002): 88.

Berger, Lance A., and Dorothy R. Berger, eds. *The Compensation Handbook*, 4th ed., New York: McGraw-Hill, 1999.

Bernardin, H. John, and R. W. Beatty. "Can Subordinates Appraisals Enhance Managerial Productivity?" *Sloan Management Review* (Summer 1987): 70-71.

Bernardin, H. John, and Richard W. Beatty. *Performance Appraisal: Assessing Human Behavior at Work.* Boston: Kent Publishing, 1984.

Bois, J. Samuel. *The Art of Awareness*, 3rd ed. Iowa: Wm. C. Brown Publishers, 1979.

Brewer, Stephen J. "Aligning Human Capital in Achieving Business Goals and Strategic Objectives." SHRM White Paper, September, 2000, Reviewed March 2002.

Brown, H. Jackson Jr., ed. *A Father's Book of Wisdom.* Tennessee: Rutledge Hill Press, 1988.

Buckingham, Marcus, and Curt Coffman. *First, Break All The Rules: What the World's Greatest Managers Do Differently.* New York: Simon and Schuster, 1999.

Butcher, David. "It Takes Two to Review." *Management Today*, (November 2002): 54-59.

Caruth, Donald L., and Gail D. Handlogten. *Managing Compensation (and Understanding It Too).* Connecticut: Quorum Books, 2001.

Cascio, Wayne F. *Managing Human Resources*, 6th ed. New York: McGraw-Hill Higher Education, 2003.

Collingwood, Harris, and Julia Kirby. *All in a Day's Work.* Boston, MA: Harvard Business Review on Breakthrough Leadership, Harvard Business School Press, 2001.

Collins James C., and Jerry I. Porras. *Building Your Company's Vision.* Boston: Harvard Business Review on Change, Harvard Business School Press, 1998.

Cornelius, N. *Human Resource Management: A Managerial Perspective*, 2nd ed. United Kingdom: Thompson Learning, 1999.

Daley, Dennis. M. *Strategic Human Resource Management-People and Performance Management in the Public Sector.* Upper Saddle River, NJ: Prentice Hall, 2002.

Daniels, Aubrey C. *Bringing Out the Best in People: How To Apply the Astonishing Power of Positive Reinforcement*. New York: McGraw-Hill, Inc., 2000.

Davis, Brian L., et al., *The Successful Manager's Handbook—Development Suggestions for Today's Managers*. Minneapolis, MN: Personnel Decisions International, 1992.

Day, David, et al. *HR Briefing*. Aspen Publishers, 1 (July 2002): 7.

DeCenzo, David A., Stephen P. Robbins. *Human Resource Management*, 6th ed. Hoboken, NJ: Wiley and Sons, Inc., 1999.

DeNisi, Angelo S., and Ricky W. Griffin. *Human Resource Management*. Massachusetts: Houghton Mifflin Company, 2001.

Dolan, Shimon L., and Denis Moran. "The Effects of Rater-Ratee Relationship on Ratee Perceptions of the Appraisal Process." *Human Resource Management*, 8th ed. New York: McGraw-Hill/Irwin, 2001.

Dreher, George R., and Thomas W. Dougherty. *Human Resource Strategy—A Behavioral Perspective for the General Manager*. New York: McGraw-Hill/Irwin, 2002.

Drucker, Peter F. *The Practice of Management*. New York: Harper Business, 1986.

Editors of The Wall Street Journal. *Boss Talk—Top CEOs Share The Ideas That Drive the World's Most Successful Companies*. New York: Random House, 2002.

Fandray, Dayton. "The New Thinking in Performance Appraisals." *Workforce* 80 (May 2001): 36.

Farkas, Charles M., and Suzy Wetlaufer. *The Way Chief Executive Officers Lead*. Boston: Harvard Business Review on Leadership, Harvard Business School Press, 1998.

Gerstner, Louis V. *Who Says Elephants Can't Dance*. New York: Harper Business, 2002.

Halpert, Jane, et al., "Pregnancy as a Source of Bias in Performance Appraisals." *Journal of Organizational Behavior* 14 (1993): 655.

Hansen, Fay. "Introduction: Experts Debate the Future of the FLSA and the NLRA." *Compensation & Benefits Review* 28, (July/August 1996): 6.

Harari, Oren. *The Leadership Secrets of Colin Powell*. New York: McGraw-Hill, 2002.

Hatfield, Shannon L. "Understanding the Four Generations to Enhance Workplace Management." *AFP Exchange* 22, (July/August 2002): 72.

Hayes, Mary. "Goal Oriented." *Information Week*, 10 (March 2003): 35.

Hays, Scott. "Pros and Cons of Pay for Performance," *ZPG* [home page on-line]; available from *http://www.zigonperf.com/resources/pmnews/proscons.html*; accessed 14 April 2003.

Heathfield, Susan. "Performance Appraisals Don't Work." *Human Resources* [home page on-line]; available from *http://humanresources.about.com/od/performanceevals/a/perf_appraisal.htm*; accessed June 2000.

Hedge, Jerry W., and Michael J. Kavanagh. "Improving the Accuracy of Performance Evaluations: Comparisons of Three Methods of Performance Appraiser Training." *Journal of Applied Psychology*, 68-73, in *Human Resource Management* (8th ed.), John M. Ivancevich, New York: McGraw-Hill/Irwin, 2001.

Hiam, Alex. *Making Horses Drink*. Irvine, CA: Entrepreneur Media, Inc., 2002.

ITAC Website and Christina Heilig. "Workshop 10—Monitoring the Program, Planning the Expansion." ITAC, 1999.

Ivancevich, John M., citing Mary N. Vinson. "The Pros and Cons of 360-Degree Feedback: Making It Work." *Training and Development* (April 1996): 11-12.

Jacoby, Sanford M. "A Century of Human Resource Management." Paper presented at the 75th Anniversary Conference of Industrial Relations Counselors, Princeton University, 11 (September 2001).

Joinson, Carla. "Managing Virtual Teams." *HRMagazine* 47 (June 2002).

Keelan, Emma. "Two for One." *Accountancy* (May 2001): 40.

Kotter, John P. "Winning at Change." *Leader to Leader*, 10 (Fall 1998): 27-33.

Kovach, Kenneth A. *Strategic Human Resources Management.* Maryland: University Press of America, 1996.

Larkin, T J, and Sandar Larkin. *Communicating Change—Winning Employee Support for New Business Goals.* New York: McGraw-Hill, Inc., 1994.

Lukas, Paul. "The Great American Company." *Fortune Small Business*, 19 (March 2003).

Mathis, Robert L., and John H Jackson. *Human Resources Management*, 10th ed. Mason, OH: South-Western College Publications, 2003.

Maxwell, John C. *The 17 Essential Qualities of A Team Player.* Tennessee: Thomas Nelson Publishers, 2002.

McKay, Matthew, et al. *Messages*, Oakland, California: New Harbinger Publications, Inc., 1995.

McKirchey, Karen. *Powerful Performance Appraisals.* Franklin Lakes, New Jersey: Career Press, 1998.

Milkovich, George T., and Jerry M. Newman. *Compensation*, 6th ed. Boston: McGraw-Hill/Irwin, 1999.

Mintzberg, Henry. *The Manager's Job.* Massachusetts: Harvard Business School Press, 1998.

Mondy, Wayne R., et al, *Human Resource Management*, 8th ed. Upper Saddle River, New Jersey: Prentice Hall, 2002.

Nelson, Bob. *1001 Ways to Reward Employees.* New York: Workman Publishing, 1994.

Newman, Edwin. *Strictly Speaking.* New York: The Bobbs-Merrill Company, 1974.

Noe, Raymond, et al. *Human Resource Management: Gaining a Competitive Advantage*, 3rd ed. New York: McGraw-Hill/Irwin, 2000.

Parks, Susan. "Improving Workplace Performance: Historical and Theoretical Contexts." *Monthly Labor Review* 20 (May 1995).

Pfeffer, Jeffrey. *Six Dangerous Myths About Pay*. Boston: Harvard Business Review on Managing People, Harvard Business School Press, 1999.

Pulakos, E.D. "The Development of Training Programs to Increase Accuracy on Different Rating Forms." *Organizational Behavior and Human Decision Processes* 38 (1986): 76-91.

Redman, T., et al. "Performance Appraisal in an NHS Hospital." *Human Resource Management Journal* 10 (2002): 48-62.

Satterfield, Terry. "Speaking of Pay." *HR Magazine* 48, (March 2003): 99-101.

Schaffer, Robert H., and Harvey A. Thomson. "Successful Change Programs begin with Results." *Harvard Business Review on Change* 70 (January 1992): 80.

Senge, Peter M. *The Fifth Discipline*. New York: Currency/Doubleday, 1994.

Smither, James W., ed. *Performance Appraisal: State of the Art in Practice*. San Francisco, CA: John Wiley & Sons, Inc., 1998.

Sujansky, Joanne. "The Critical Care and Feeding of Generation Y," *Workforce* (May 2002): 15.

Swan, William S. *How To Do a Superior Performance Appraisal*. New York: John Wiley & Sons, 1991.

Tannen, Dr. Deborah. *That's Not What I Meant*. New York: Ballantine Books, 1986.

Toffler, Alvin. *Powershift*. New York: Bantam Books, Bantam Doubleday Dell Publishing Group, 1990.

Wah, Louisa. "Managing Gen Xers Strategically." *Management Review* 89 (March 2000): 6.

Woods, Robert H. *Managing Hospitality Human Resources*, 3rd ed. Lansing, MI: Educational Institute of the American Hotel and Lodging Association, 2002.

Zemke, Ron, and Susan Zemke. "30 Things We Know For Sure About Adult Learning." *Training/HRD Magazine* (June 1981).

Index

About the Author

Sharon Armstrong began her career in human resources in 1985 as a recruiter/trainer in a large Manhattan law firm. Since then, she has served as a Director of Human Resources at another law firm and three nonprofit associations in Washington, D.C. Her responsibilities always included oversight of the performance management system.

Since launching her consulting business, Sharon Armstrong and Associates, in 1998, Armstrong has consulted with many large corporations and small businesses. She has provided training and completed human resource projects dealing with performance management design and implementation for a wide variety of clients in the profit and nonprofit sectors, as well as government settings. She received her bachelor's degree from the University of Southern Maine and her master's degree in counseling from George Washington University. She is a certified Professional in Human Resources.

Sharon is the coauthor of a humor book, *Heeling the Canine Within: The Dog's Self-Help Companion*, and two business books, *Stress-free Performance Appraisals* and *The Essential HR Handbook*.